The Way I Was

The Way I Was

Marvin Hamlisch

WITH GERALD GARDNER

INTEGRATED MEDIA
NEW YORK

This work is a memoir. It reflects the author's present recollections of his experiences over a period of years. Some names and identifying characteristics have been changed in order to protect the identity of certain individuals. Any resulting resemblance to persons living or dead is entirely coincidental and unintentional.

ISBN: 978-1-5040-9674-4

This edition published in 2024 by Open Road Integrated Media, Inc.
180 Maiden Lane
New York, NY 10038
www.openroadmedia.com

To the memory of my beloved parents

To Terre

CONTENTS

A NOTE FROM THE AUTHOR

Picture this. Little Marvin, age six, is ushered into his admissions test for the Juilliard School of Music. There I am, in my Sailor Boy's suit, facing three tall men. (Everybody looks tall when you're six.)

A professor asks:

"Marvin, will you be playing any Mozart for us? Or possibly Clementi?"

"No," I said. "I don't know who Clementi is. And I never studied Mozart."

"Then what *will* you be playing for us?"

"Well, I listen to the radio a lot. I can play 'Goodnight Irene.'"

The professor pondered.

"Well, I don't *know* 'Goodnight Irene,'" he said.

"That's all right," says Little Marvin. "I can play it in any key you want."

And so I proceeded to play the song in every key the professor named. And those were the keys that opened the lock to the Juilliard School of Music.

Come to think of it, I don't recall anyone ever asking, "Marvin, do you want to take piano lessons?" My father, a musician himself, recognized that I had musical talent. By three, I would keep time to the music on the radio in our apartment. By the time I was five, when my sister took her piano lessons, I would listen from the kitchen, and when her teacher left, I would go to the piano and pick out all the songs by ear. Everyone saw in me some sort of wunderkind whose talents had to be served. Given all this, my father felt it his duty to launch me on a career as a great concert pianist. The problem was, that was his dream, not mine.

So from age six to twenty I attended a school where I unfailingly threw up before every final exam. I was terrified that I'd betray my father's hopes. And for fourteen years I competed with a pack of driven young kids who wanted to become the next Horowitz. Me, I wanted to become the next Cole Porter. Unfortunately, there were no classes in this hallowed institution where one could learn how to write a Broadway show; no Berlin 101 or Rodgers 202.

As the Juilliard years dragged by, I concealed my true tastes like a spy behind enemy lines. I lived in fear that my guilty secret would be discovered. No one at Juilliard must know that I loved Jerome Kern and Harold Arlen. By age seven, in our tiny apartment on West Eighty-first Street, I was banging out my own pop tunes. Windows flanked the piano, so whatever I wrote was audible to the world. Even then I worried that if a cab was waiting at the light, the driver might shout up at me: "Hey, kid, that's a loser."

Cabbie be damned. I wasn't going to give up my dream of composing for the theatre. I'd show 'em. Just give me another year or two. I was a kid in a hurry. But it took much longer than that. I spent the next thirteen years at Juilliard becoming proficient at playing Bach and Beethoven, hoping all along that I'd spend most of my life playing Hamlisch.

Yet years later, with my parents gone, I still heard the voice of my father looking down at me from some celestial plane, with the music of Mozart in the background, saying: "What's the matter, Marvin? By the time Gershwin was your age, he was dead. And he'd written a *concerto*. Where's *your* concerto, Marvin?" Eerily, it was a question that continued to haunt me even after I had won my Oscars for *The Way We Were* and *The Sting* and had written the music for *A Chorus Line*.

This book is not an autobiography in the conventional sense. How could it be? I feel as if there's still as much yet to be done as has already been done. Besides, I never imagined that one day I might be asked to write a book like this, so I never made notes, kept a diary (only for *A Chorus Line*), or saved letters. So let's call this a collection of recollections, some good, some not so good, some about my family and the friends I've made along the way, and some of the work I've done. The music I've played and music I've written trigger memories. "Mem-ries, light the corners of my mind . . ."

Hmm, I think there's a song in that.

The Way I Was

1.

MUSIC LESSONS

I know there are more gifted people than me out there. But they may not make it in the music world even if they have the talent, because they don't have the desire and the ego to drive themselves as hard as they can. Or because they've gotten derailed along the line and can't find their way back to their real goals. Or because they didn't have the parents I had to foster their talents.

Well, I may have had the ego, the drive, and the gift, but I also had *parents who fostered like crazy*. They fostered me to the school that probably has educated more modern-day musicians than any other—the Juilliard School of Music. You have to understand more about my parents to know why they enrolled me in the Preparatory Division at age six, the youngest student ever to walk those hallowed halls. They were from Vienna, and my father, Max, would have certainly stayed there if Hitler hadn't had other ideas. Max loved Vienna and was a true Viennese gentleman—the sort who kissed ladies' hands. He loved Old World culture, the music of Schubert, Schumann, Strauss, the cafés, the incredible desserts. But by the mid-thirties, he had a keen sense that it was time for those Jews who could to get out of Europe. My father had been on his way to a successful career as a musician in Vienna, but it was short-circuited by the sudden move to a place where a new language was a barrier.

Arriving in America and not being fluent in English, he found it hard to cope with this frantic new land. Like most Viennese, instead of trying to adapt to New York, he decided to replicate Vienna here. Because he was from the old school, institutions of learning were everything to him. This meant nothing less than his son achieving the success that had been denied him by the fateful march of history.

In his eyes, Juilliard was where God learned to play the scales, and if Juilliard was good enough for God, it just might be good enough for Marvin Frederick Hamlisch, born June 2, 1944. So when the letter arrived to say that Max's six-year-old son had been accepted, you would have thought it had come from Ed McMahon, saying we had won the first prize in the Publishers Clearing House giveaway. My father was instantly transformed from a poor Austrian immigrant into the impossibly proud father of a Juilliard student. Was I really the dedicated music student who had a burning desire to play classical music? Well, no. Was I merely a kid who needed musical training? Well, yes.

By the ripe old age of seven, having spent one year at Juilliard, I knew I was never going to be a great concert pianist. Juilliard's primary intention was to make their students great instrumentalists, and anything else, like composing for the theatre, was not for them. Juilliard was going to make me the next Horowitz whether I liked it or not. But I did not want to practice that much; I didn't have the technical ability or confidence. I was much too nervous for it. I would throw up before every recital. There was not a men's room in the six floors of Juilliard that had not seen the pale, quivering form of young Mr. Hamlisch. Before every recital, I would look down at the back of my hands and see the vivid blue of my bulging veins like a road map to terror. It was a very competitive surrounding in which I found myself, and the jittery nerves and acid stomach that have dogged me ever since began at that school.

I took piano lessons once a week from Edgar Roberts, the teacher Juilliard assigned me, at his apartment on 103rd Street and Riverside Drive. I also attended P.S. 9 from nine to three each day, and then on Saturday, while my friends were playing stickball, I'd report to Juilliard, where I attended classes in theory, sight reading, and harmony. Mind you, I am not pleading child abuse. I did see Hopalong Cassidy on TV and played my share of stickball. I adapted and developed a new philosophy. I was only going to dread one day at a time.

To lighten the load when I practiced at home, I would mix in some rock and roll that I'd heard on the radio. My father was chagrined to hear the rock with the Beethoven, but my mother convinced him not to scold. Actually, I gave him no cause for complaint. It all came easily to me, and year after year, my scholarship was renewed. In fact, against all the odds, I beat out the dedicated "culture vultures" and won the coveted school contest. First prize was that you got to perform in front of a packed house at Town Hall. I personally would have preferred cash. Or a trip to Maui.

If I practiced one hour daily, that was a lot. But after that hour there was plenty of time to play songs I heard or songs I wrote. From the time I could play the piano, I remember trying to write tunes. They were in my head, and I would just sit down and start noodling. Next thing I knew, I had written a melody. My first opus was called "Billy-Boy." ("One day I was a-walking / To find my Billy-Boy / He was gone, / He was gone, / He was gone." Don't worry. I know. That's enough. Even then, I knew I would need a lyricist.) None of this seemed out of the ordinary to me. It's like standard equipment on a car.

Frankly, as long as I can remember, I loved writing songs. If I couldn't play a Chopin nocturne as well as Horowitz or some kid in my class, then it seemed that all this intense training to become a great pianist was absurd. But that didn't stop my father from repeating over and over: "Practice, Marvin, practice." I had to invent an assortment of excuses to get up from "*Für Elise*." Still, how many times can you go to the bathroom? ("Max," my mother would cry, "I think Marvin has a bladder infection.")

My father by now could tell there was something lacking in my dedication. So he concocted a scheme to turn lemons into lemonade. He created a card game. (Maybe I should sell the rights to Parker Brothers.) He designed a homemade deck of cards. He took out a protractor and measured the cards so they'd be the same size as official playing cards. And on the back of each one it would say MARVIN (my first big credit). And on the face side it said PRACTICE THE CHOPIN FOR 15 MINUTES or DO G-FLAT MAJOR SCALE. I would pick a card and have to follow the directions on it. The trick was, there was one card marked TEN-MINUTE BREAK. Of course, unknown to my father, I had marked the cards. I knew where that break card was all the time. Eventually, I was found out, but for a brief, shining moment, I had committed the perfect crime.

Sometimes the scheduling of Saturday music classes left me hours of waiting time between them. Rather than travel from 122nd Street and Broadway (where Juilliard used to be in those days) to our apartment and back, I would hunt for one of the practice rooms at school. A lot of the other students also sought out these rooms to get in some extra study. Pianists, cellists, violists roamed the halls in wolf packs. These rooms had double doors. The idea was that if you were playing the piano loudly, the flutist next door wouldn't be disturbed. On those days when

I was lucky enough to find a practice room, I knew that the room to my right was probably being used by a brilliant protégé working feverishly on a difficult Beethoven sonata. The room to my left, no doubt, had some eight-year-old Japanese violinist perfecting some ultracomplicated cadenza. Both of them oblivious to the fact that I was playing "Tears on my Pillow," a fifties rock-and-roll song. If the faculty had heard me, there would have been tears on *my* pillow.

There I'd be, playing just because I loved to play, and thanks to those miraculous double doors, my guilty secret remained mine alone. Marvin, the fugitive musician, player and composer of pop tunes. By now, I had hidden away a stackful of my own songs. Those doors helped me conceal my decadent tastes. Mind you, I am not suggesting that you adopt a life of deception, concealment, and misrepresentation. But it's always worked for me.

Once a year every Juilliard student took an examination in his or her proficiency at their instrument. The test would determine whether you kept your scholarship for the following year. In my case, it was an absolute must, since my parents couldn't afford the tuition. The exam took place in front of the people they called the Jury. (Has a nice ring to it: like "convicted on all counts.")

The annual recital exam always came shortly after my birthday and totally soiled the event. If the exam was on June 4, it would render my birthday on the second a disaster. How could you enjoy cake, cookies, and presents when two days later you would have to face the firing squad? For the examination, you had to present a typewritten list of the pieces you were prepared to play, enter a windowless room that had nothing in it but a piano and three judges, hand them the list, and stand there in agony, waiting till they decided what they wanted to hear. They usually chose the most difficult part of each piece. Naturally. But for me there was an even bigger problem. Presenting them with the typewritten list proved formidable in itself. We didn't own a typewriter.

I'd usually begin the day of the exam by throwing up. And that was the high point of the day. (It never got any better in the fourteen years I attended Juilliard.) My mother would give me nothing but weak chamomile tea, or I would sip shot glasses of Maalox. I would think about the hours after the exam when I'd be able to join my friends and play baseball. There would be no further need to protect my hands. The summer would come, and I'd be free till September. But freedom passed quickly, and before I knew it, it was time to survive another examination and then be allowed to return to the hallowed halls.

The worst examination recital I can remember was at age ten. My mother bought me my first gray wool suit for the occasion from Rappoport's at Eighty-third and Broadway. The day of my exam was the first day I had actually worn the suit, and I suddenly realized that I could never play the Kabalevsky E-Flat Major Sonata or anything else, because the pants itched too much. The wool was driving me nuts. But as usual, my mother had a solution. There was no time to get another suit and no time to stitch a lining in this one.

"Marvin, put on your pajama bottoms underneath. The ones with the little bears and Indians." All day, along with my usual dread of flunking the exam and losing my scholarship (and my breakfast), I carried the secret fear that my humiliating pajama-pants secret would somehow be discovered.

But that day had greater terrors in store. My father, always a cautious man, insisted we leave the house with ample time to spare. So we arrived at school with a full hour to kill. The waiting was hell. To help me through the interminable sixty minutes, my father decided we would explore the Juilliard building. That was a little like taking Anne Boleyn on a tour of the Tower to keep her mind off what lay ahead.

First we paced the hallways of Juilliard's six floors. Then we explored a few empty classrooms. Then we bought some pencils at Schirmer's music store downstairs. Then we examined the bulletin boards. Unfortunately, all of this only used up about ten minutes. But the diversion was working. I had not thrown up, and I was actually settling down. My father's plan of coming to school this early had its pluses: I was blinking much more slowly.

"Tell you what, Marvin. Let's go up on the roof. It's a beautiful day." It seemed like a great idea. I had wolfed down a handful of Maalox tablets and felt pretty good. Father and son strolling on the roof—what could be nicer?

We took in the glories of New York, looking across at Grant's Tomb, which stood nearby. I couldn't help but wonder if Grant's Tomb was the final resting place of some Juilliard student named Grant who failed the exam. Back came the nerves. My father quieted me down, and we started to talk.

Finally, I got brave enough to ask:

"Daddy, why do I have to go to Juilliard?"

"Marvin, I know this is hard for you, but you can't give up. God gave you a talent—you mustn't waste it. I know you can do it." He told me over and over that I had been given this gift and that to waste it would let down God, my parents, and myself. I began to understand why, for him, it was so important for me to stick with this. Unlike my father, I wasn't going to be driven out of my homeland.

"God has not just given you your talent, Marvin," he said. "He's put you in a land where you know the language, a place where no one can take success away from you." I nodded.

"Marvin, you are probably too young to understand this. What I'm giving you is a rare thing. I never had the chance myself. Here in this building there's a foundation you're getting that will stay with you forever. Musical training has to start young. It has to get into your blood. Over and over and over, practice, practice, practice. Marvin," he said lovingly, "I know you like to write songs, and the better the pianist you are, the better you can play them. Years from now, you'll know what all this means." Then he kissed me on the forehead.

I looked down at my watch and saw that the time had flown. There were only five minutes to go. The talk with my father had calmed me down. I felt fine. I could face the Jury and play my best. I had not thrown up. I was in command. I was ready.

We headed for the door to the roof. It was locked.

Instant hysteria. The Jury waited below. My moment of truth had arrived, and I was up on the roof, struggling with a locked iron door. I beat my little fists on it, but to no avail. We ran to the edge of the roof, leaned far over, and I started to shout at the top of my lungs: "Help! Help!" I was perspiring into my new woolen suit, and father and son were overcome by panic. Finally, we attracted somebody's attention on the street, and after enough time to turn a confident student into a raving maniac, the superintendent arrived to open the door.

When I reached the Jury twenty-five minutes late, I was a pathetic sight. My hands were covered with soot, my pajama pants were drenched with sweat, my nerves were shot. Other than that, it was just another spring day in Manhattan. I handed the three typewritten, now slightly wrinkled sheets to the jurors. After I had played a few mandatory scales, they asked me to play some of the Kabalevsky. But as I raised my fingers above the keyboard, I heard a titter from one of the jurors. Then I heard a laugh from another. I was concentrating with all my might on the sonata, and as I had been taught, I kept my eyes on the keys. But as I looked downward, I saw the little orange bears and Indians peeking out of the cuffs of my pants, staring up at me.

Well, I passed the dreaded annual exam and won the right to do it again next year. I love happy endings.

I am a great believer in the jury system, but not for six-year-olds. Looking back on those yearly days of pain and panic, I really don't believe that the mind of a young child is designed to handle this kind of pressure. My parents looked on the stress of those exams as they looked on a polio shot—a necessary and transitory discomfort. To think, at such an early age you are already auditioning. You have to prove that you are "good enough." Otherwise you're replaced, losing your scholarship to a more ambitious child and, in so doing, disgracing your parents. You experience tension, anguish, fear, all the things that make life worth living.

Yet, you might not believe this, but if I had to do it again, I'd do it—not just because Juilliard gave me the training I would later draw on as a composer, pianist, and conductor. I'd do it for those fifty minutes on the roof and the time alone with my father. The examination was hell, but those fifty minutes with Max Hamlisch were sheer heaven.

2.

ELBOW ROOM

I have spent more time with the piano than with anybody. I have always felt comfortable around it, and it seems like my oldest friend. It's one reason why I can give a concert in one city, fly to another, and feel perfectly at home when I step onstage. Because there it is, my old buddy, the piano. A piano can be a protective armor against the world. It seemed like that to me even in the first grade at P.S. 9 on Eighty-second Street and Broadway. I was the type of kid with a perpetual nervous stomach, frightened to be alone and constantly in need of someone to cling to.

My father was busy trying to make a living with his accordion, so my mother was elected as my ubiquitous protector and confidante. In those days my father sought jobs at a mysterious place called "the union," a meeting hall for members of Musicians Union 802. He usually did this in the afternoon, worked at night, and came home in the early hours of the morning. Therefore, I saw him mostly on weekends and at dinnertime. I saw a lot more of my mother—from the instant I awoke, when she was assembling my lunch box, and when I returned from P.S. 9 at three o'clock.

In the first grade I had a teacher named Miss Morrison who I remember as a cross between Eva Braun and the Wicked Witch of the West. In the mornings I was especially nervous about the whole harrowing day that stretched ahead, when I left my mother and went off to encounter my classroom nemesis. I had little stomach for breakfast, so my mother would give me a packet of Social Tea biscuits to eat at the eleven o'clock milk break. But when you've skipped breakfast because of a tense colon, your appetite comes early.

To this day, friends know that when I get hungry, my whole personality changes. Beware the hand that doesn't feed a ravenous Marvin Hamlisch. So as Miss Morrison tried to drive home the finer points of Jack, Jill, and their dog, Spot, I felt faint and furious. Like an addict, I dove for the only thing that could satisfy my cravings. I needed those cookies. Unfortunately, it was only 10:00 A.M.

"Marvin," Miss Morrison bellowed, "you cannot eat before the rest of the class. You will have to wait till eleven." She made it sound like the Eleventh Commandment.

So I kicked her. You heard me, I kicked Miss Morrison very hard in the ankle, right through her orthopedic stockings.

I realize that nowadays, when there can be a switchblade in every pencil case, kicking a teacher may not seem like much. But to me, at that time and in that community, I could see the headlines in the *New York Post*: "No Pardon from Governor for Mad Kicker." And I knew this would be an enormous embarrassment to my parents, particularly my father. We might have been living in New York, but his values were pure Vienna, and the idea of assaulting someone who was giving you an education, well, that was unthinkable. No sooner did I commit my heinous crime than, horrified by my deed and its implications, I raced for home and told my mother what I had done. She was, as usual, loving and supportive.

"Don't worry, darling," she said. "Everything will be all right. I know you must feel very sorry. Right now it seems like a terrible thing. But you'll have a nice glass of milk and a couple of doughnuts, and then, when your father gets home, he'll kill you."

My mother didn't have to tell me. I knew, with the wonderful wisdom of children, that my father would not be as forbearing as my mother. I knew that once my father, with his obsession about authority, arrived home, Little Marvin would be in deep trouble. Punishment and retribution were on the way. The world was in the state it was because Hitler invaded Poland, Mussolini murdered Ethiopians, and Marvin Hamlisch kicked his teacher. So, filled with contrition and fear, I did the prudent, sensible, logical thing.

I hid in a suitcase.

Since the suitcase was smack in the middle of the living-room floor, you might feel that I wasn't thinking clearly. Yet I felt confident my father would never find me in this well-conceived hiding place. This is *not* an example of the wonderful wisdom of children.

My father found me. It didn't take him long. First he looked in the closet, then in the piano, then in the suitcase. Bingo.

Now, if my mother would hit me, it would be *with* something. Like the *New York Herald Tribune*. Or the *Daily Mirror*. It made a difference. It was more admonitory than painful. When she smacked me with the *New York Times Book Review* section, you could even say it was instructive. But when my father heard that I had kicked my teacher—actually *kicked* her—something snapped. I had done something unpardonable, and now he did something that for him was unthinkable. He only hit me once in my life, and this was it. I still remember that moment. It was a terrible shock.

My mother dealt with the problem in a totally different way.

She realized that my frustration lay in my being terribly hungry and being nervous at leaving her side. I had coped with kindergarten, all right, but Miss Morrison was a whole new ball game. My mother decided I needed to be weaned away from her apron strings rather than going cold turkey into Miss Morrison's clutches each morning, so from then on, she started coming to school with me every day—and staying.

She would bring me to P.S. 9 each morning, then, undaunted, she settled into a chair in the corridor outside the classroom. No matter what Miss Morrison would do or say to me, I would have the comforting knowledge that my mother was nearby. In fact, whenever I felt the least bit insecure, I was allowed to leave my little seat, cross to the door, and satisfy myself that she was still out there. My mother's vigil continued for three months, and during the last month, it slowly melted away. Her sentry duty was first cut to three hours a day, then ninety minutes, then an hour, and finally, she wasn't out there anymore.

But I had *kicked* Miss Morrison, and the Board of Education of the City of New York had neither forgiven nor forgotten. The school had labeled me a "truant," and my parents received a solemn letter to that effect. They were informed that I would require regular sessions with a guidance counselor. It was to this official that school principals sent their problem children. What a stigma. My future was hopelessly tainted—six years old and reporting to a guidance counselor. Next stop, the parole board. The school must have had a grim scenario mapped out for me.

Now here's the part of the story that proves the maxim "When God shuts a door, He opens a window." It's the part that led to the bond of friendship between me and my piano; where the piano lifted me from the miasma of crime and made me a useful member of society.

Despite the terror of what awaited me, the guidance counselor turned out to be a terrific guy. He gave me interesting things to do in his office, like letting me play with his stopwatch. That I loved. To me he was "The Stopwatch Doctor." (Any students of irony will want to note that twenty-five years later, a stopwatch would become my basic tool in scoring Hollywood movies.) My father, seeing the pleasure the stopwatch gave me, promptly bought me my own so that I could play with it at home.

Meanwhile, we concluded our sessions, and I was returned to a productive life in the classroom, a truant no more. My time with the guidance counselor was over. He even recommended that I be allowed to eat some cookies in class if I was hungry. To this day, therapists call this the Duncan Hines Theory of Child Psychology.

Dr. Stopwatch, in his infinite wisdom, detected that I had definite musical talent. He came to my rescue. He insisted that I be given every opportunity to use my musical talent at P.S. 9 Miraculously, an old upright materialized in my classroom. Dr. Stopwatch had said, in effect, "Give this boy a piano," and they did. Rehabilitation had reached the Mad Kicker. That bit of percipient advice changed my life. Because he urged the authorities to give me "things to do with music," my school days brightened like an Oklahoma cornfield. My friend the piano and I were never going to be separated again. This effected a giant change in the way I related to school, a transformation not unlike preparing Eliza Doolittle for the embassy ball.

When the second grade began, the upright was moved into my new classroom. Miss Morrison was gone, and my new teacher was Miss Sussman. (Give the role to a redheaded Donna Reed.) My mother was no longer in the hall, and I had turned into the Leonard Bernstein of Eighty-second Street—pianist, musician, composer, all-purpose music man. A good deal of attention was being paid to me, and I was churning out a lot of music. Every time there was an assembly, those noisy gatherings in the auditorium, Little Marvin was onstage at the piano. Oh, the power. Oh, the prestige. One G seventh chord, and four hundred students and teachers would rise as one from their seats. Then I'd hit 'em with the national anthem, and four hundred voices would burst into song. But the part that really showed my influence was when I played a C major chord, letting them sit. I mean, without that chord, nobody moved. I felt like General Patton shouting, "At ease!" to the 3rd Army Corps. I was the School Piano Player, able to leap tall octaves in a single bound. If I had heard of Andy Warhol, I would have told him my fifteen minutes of fame had arrived.

During this heady period, I was assigned other jobs that were not as musical but were also associated with the arts. The guidance counselor had urged that I be kept busy at all times to harness my nervous energy. So I was often posted in the paint closet and given the job of handing out paints to other students. This was not the ideal assignment, since I have always been color-blind. I can make out the yellows, but the greens and browns look pretty much alike. The kids drew some pretty bizarre flowers that year. This became known as my blue period.

When I went from the second grade to the third, a curious thing happened. Miss Sussman was promoted along with me, and so was the upright. This was either the kind act of providence or the school's decision to keep me neutralized at all costs. In any case, I remained under Miss Sussman's benign influence for a second year. What's more, she loved show business and Broadway shows. There followed a jumble of class musicals, rehearsals, and choirs, with me at the piano for all of them. The outsider of earlier years had turned into the ultimate team player. I was aglow in the favorable attention of teachers and students alike. Especially Nina Tumarkin, a blond classmate of mine. Nina was a product of God at His very best. (But that's another story.)

By the time I reached the sixth grade, I was playing the piano rather well. I not only played the pieces I was taught by Mr. Roberts, my teacher at Juilliard (where I continued throwing up on a pretty regular basis), but I could really play "by ear" most of the songs I heard on the radio. All I had to do was hear a piece of music a few times and I could pick out the tune immediately. I also had perfect pitch, another goody that God threw into the bargain. When someone played a note, I instantly knew what it was, an A or G or E-flat or whatever. Coupled with playing by ear, I could play any song I heard, in any key. You may wonder what it's like with perfect pitch and a good ear. I've always wondered what it's like *without* them. I mean, I'm one of the few people who goes to a movie and hears the music instead of the dialogue.

With my ability to play both classical music and show tunes, I was sure on the way. My first parlor performance came at the request of my beloved Miss Sussman. I remember she cornered me one June day toward the end of the school year. She had a flattering suggestion. She proposed to hire me to play the piano at a party she was giving at her home for some teacher friends. She was even going to pay me. I eagerly looked forward to the upcoming weekend. I even had a suit that didn't itch.

The school year was nearly over, the dreaded Juilliard exam was behind me, and the weather was sunny and warm. So the day before the party, I donned some ragged blue jeans and went outside to do what I loved to do—*play ball*. In case you missed the chance to grow up on the streets of Manhattan, I should point out the sociological oddity that New York City streets are actually ball fields. On West Eighty-first Street between

Columbus and Amsterdam avenues, the lamppost serves as first base, the sewer manhole is second, the church steps are third, and wherever you want is home.

Now, in this pickup game of baseball, I was the catcher. This was a singularly hazardous position. You will never see a photograph of Leonard Bernstein playing catcher, and there's a very good reason, which I was about to learn. The leadoff batter was overzealous. Or maybe I was too close to home plate. History is unclear on this point. The batter swung heroically at the first pitch and missed. The bat's momentum carried it around and struck me in the left eye. If the trajectory of this swing had been a half inch lower, I would now be starring in pirate movies. But I could see no silver lining at the time. Matter of fact, I could see very little.

I hurried home to show my mother the Mount Everest that was growing on my eyebrow. To this day, I clearly remember two things about my mother in this crisis. First, the look of pure horror on her face as I walked into the kitchen. Second, the cool, methodical way in which she dealt with calamity. These two extremes of emotion—horror and efficiency—define for me the wonder that is motherhood.

She took the flat end of a knife and pressed the protuberance down with both hands, at the same time that she was putting ice on the eye. Yes, she had three hands. The next day, I had what you call a real shiner. I looked as if I had gone six rounds with Marciano. All right, make it thirty seconds with Mickey Rourke. What was uppermost in my ten-year-old mind, once the pain subsided, was that I didn't want to let my teacher down. The following evening, I was to play the Sussman living room. She was *counting* on me.

My mother tried her best to disguise the lump. She put a pancake base on the swelling, but it was still distended and discolored. But the show must go on. At the appointed hour I entered the Sussman domicile. My eye was a rhapsody in purple. A roomful of respectable teachers gasped when they saw my ravaged face. Miss Sussman ran to me.

"Good Lord," she said. "Who hit you?"

The teachers oohed and aahed their liberal biases, and I never got the chance to explain that I owed my wound to Abner Doubleday, not to some young Bugsy Siegel. I crossed to the piano bench, sat down, and poured out a medley of pop and Broadway music for the appreciative guests. Think of it—a new category for the Oscars: "Best Performance by a Child Pianist in a Living Room with a Black Eye."

Guests looked on with expressions that said, "How brave of the little fellow to carry on. Such courage—and so talented." Jimmy Breslin says that a conservative is a liberal who has been mugged. That evening, I'm afraid I turned a lot of nice liberal schoolteachers into right-wing vigilantes.

Our sixth-grade class at P.S. 9 put on a production of *H.M.S. Pinafore*. By now I was in charge, an eleven-year-old impresario. I taught the songs, rehearsed the cast, shortened certain parts, and played all the music. (And polished up the handle of the big front door.) I guess you'd say this was my first experience with mounting a show, and I loved it all, and it all came naturally.

It was at about this time that the young man who was later to marry my sister began to play an important role in my life. Howard Liebling was my mother's brother's wife's brother. (Got that?) He became my first lyricist, and so the twenty-seven-year-old Howard and the eleven-year-old Marvin formed an unlikely collaboration that would soon produce more than a few songs.

In our bathroom we had a little radio that I kept tuned to WABC, where a DJ called Cousin Brucie regularly played the top-forty hits. This kept me wired into the sounds of the day, but it produced an unhealthy effect on my composing. My songs sounded uncannily like whatever I heard. If one morning I was brushing my teeth to something romantic called "I Love You, Baby," I would shortly come up with a romantic rock song called "I *Really* Love You, Baby." I was the ultimate chameleon composer—a veritable Zelig of the keyboard. With Howard at my side, we turned out dozens of songs and spent hours scheming about how we would get our big break.

If our apartment was a little cramped for four energetic people, the addition of Howard Liebling's daily visits to my sister, and my music, made our living arrangements downright eccentric. Apartment 2E was the only one I had ever known, so to me it all seemed practical and conventional. My sister, Terry, and I slept in the living room. She slept on a convertible sofa, and I slept on a narrow box spring and mattress. We were separated by a chest of drawers that preserved a fragile sense of privacy. My box spring was a step from the closet where I kept all my possessions and a step from the piano in the other direction. What could be more convenient?

Then there was the kitchen, where we ate all our meals. We spent a lot of time in there, but I can never recall seeing my mother actually sitting down. Serving food and hovering at the stove, yes—but sitting down, never. My mother was a cook for all seasons and all hours. My father would often return home at 3:00 A.M. from playing accordion at a private party. My mother would be sound asleep as he approached our front door, but when his key slid into the lock, somehow she knew that her "Maxel" was home. In no time flat she would be in the kitchen whipping up a meal worthy of a Viennese chef. None of your turkey on rye, either; it would be veal cutlets and spaetzle at 3:15 A.M. By then Terry and I were wide awake and had joined the festivities. My father would present us with the dessert he had brought home from the hotel where he had played that night.

I'll never forget the cupboard in our kitchen that defied one of the basic laws of physics. Two things seemed to occupy the same space at the same time. Since there was only one cupboard, cans of soup huddled against light bulbs, and cereal boxes abutted masking tape. I can't say I ever saw the back wall of that cabinet. It was like God: you assumed His existence though you hadn't really seen Him.

My mother had come from Austria to America, a conservative Jew. Her religion was sacred to her. Even in Vienna, when the Gestapo had hauled her in for questioning, she secretly kept her Jewish star around her neck, under her blouse. She never removed it. My father warned her: "Lilly, take it off. It's too dangerous to wear in the streets." But my mother told him: "No. Never."

It wasn't that she demanded that her children be religious, but she instilled it in us by her example. I think we followed in her footsteps because she made us see the truth of God in the way she lived her life. She was a street fighter with the best of them but always humble in her Jewishness. Four holidays were especially significant in our house: Passover, Chanukah, Rosh Hashanah, and Yom Kippur. The last two were so meaningful that I always attended the services; working on those holy days was unthinkable. Every year, when my mother got a calendar, she'd instantly circle the dates of these two holidays. To this day I do the same thing.

My mother and father were very different people. She was an assertive, pragmatic woman whose favorite saying was "You've got to make elbows," by which she meant: In this bustling world of self-absorbed people, you have to make yourself a little elbow room. My father, on the other hand, was more cautious and pessimistic.

Let me give you an example: My sister and I loved to attend the Macy's Thanksgiving Day Parade, which moved down Central Park West a few blocks from our apartment house. As parade time approached on Thanksgiving Day, it was almost impossible to get to Central Park West. The crowds were thick, and after a certain time the men in blue prevented anyone else from approaching the parade route. Often, the Hamlisch family, which liked their beauty sleep, was late arriving.

Once, when a policeman standing by a wooden barrier barred our way, my father shrugged and said, "Yes, yes, I understand." He was ready to turn back. But my mother's eyes widened.

"Officer," she said, "we're not going to the parade. We've got an appointment at Dr. Ehrlinger's office," and she pointed toward Central Park West. (Every year at Thanksgiving, we had turkey and this white lie served up on a platter.) The policeman, clearly outsmarted, waved us through.

"See?" my mother said as we took our places on the parade route. "You've got to make elbows."

And so you do.

The memories of my mother tending my baseball wound and waiting outside my classroom, of my father helping me walk off the tension on the Juilliard roof, remain vivid and indelible. But this may be the time for you to get to know something of their history before I came their way.

My mother, Lilly Schachter, was born in Vienna and trained as a seamstress. She left school after the third grade because her mother was ill and she had to care for her. Lilly was a beautiful girl and the target of every eligible male in the inner city. One of these was a handsome, wealthy young fellow with the musical-comedy name of Ernst Pickholtz. My mother's family was all for her marrying Ernst immediately because, with the clouds of Nazism approaching Austria, Ernst could whisk her off to Argentina. If he had, she wouldn't have had to escape the storm troopers in the precarious way she did, and today I would be Marvin Pickholtz, composer of *Evita*.

The only downside to Ernst Pickholtz was that my mother was already in love with another man, a musician named Max Hamlisch. But he lacked the financial means to get her out of Vienna. It was the old story of a woman choosing between love and Buenos Aires.

My father had studied to be a commercial artist, but his first love was music, and he barely scraped by playing at dances. He married my mother and they moved into a small apartment on the Pillersdorfgasse. They would have undoubtedly remained there and lived happily ever after, with "The Blue Danube Waltz" for underscoring, except for Adolf Hitler.

By 1935, Max knew in his bones, it was time to go. As I mentioned, long before many others realized it, my father could see the writing on the wall, that Hitler was not just a Charlie Chaplin look-alike, that *der Führer* had an appetite for conquest and Austria was high on his menu. But it is one thing to know you should leave a place and another to walk away from your home and friends and way of life.

And where was he to go? One day, a musician friend told my father of a job that was available in the Wald Hotel in the town of Vaduz, across the border in Liechtenstein. This was the postage-stamp-sized country immortalized by Irving Berlin in *Call Me Madam*. My father was allowed to commute by train, and he carried papers that were stamped HEIL HITLER. Unbelievably, the Wald Hotel was a favorite watering hole of the Nazi SS; thankfully, they listened to the Jewish accordionist more than they looked at him.

This job was to become the stepping-stone for my parents' escape from Austria. Only my father had official papers; my mother didn't. In order to get them, she had to present herself at an office and wait in a line, FOR JEWS ONLY, and in these ghoulish times, that had its dangers. But my mother made elbows. With the guts and nerve that had always distinguished her, she put herself in the line for ARYANS. But it was to no avail. The line was endless, and there were no documents to be had.

So each day my father commuted to his job by train, and each day the pressures on Austrian Jews continued to build. My parents' escape from Austria was completely serendipitous, as so many important changes in life seem to be. On the train to his job at the Wald Hotel, my father carried all his instruments with him. He played several, which meant every evening he traveled back and forth with a flute, a clarinet, a saxophone, and an accordion. Being a gregarious fellow, he often took out his accordion on the train and played for the other passengers and was soon accepted as one of the commuting regulars.

My mother packed a small suitcase for him each night. Packing was one of the things she did better than any living person. If there were a Nobel Prize for packing, she would have won it. She had the ability to cram three suitcases' worth of things into one. Not a cubic inch went unused. Toothbrushes slid into shirt pockets, and alarm clocks went into slippers along with socks and underwear. How many times did she send me off on a trip with one suitcase and I'd have to buy two more to bring all my things home again?

My mother felt that no valise was meticulously packed unless it contained a few pieces of fruit to ward off the ravages of hunger. Because my father loved grapefruit, my mother always packed a big one for him. Her dilemma was: Where do you put a grapefruit without consuming space? A peach goes in a shoe; a banana goes in a sock. But a grapefruit? Her solution was to ram it into the bell of his saxophone.

One night on the train, the conductor warned my father: "Max, this train is not going to Liechtenstein. We've been rerouted to Germany. They're starting to arrest Jews. When the train starts to slow down, that's the signal: That's the time to jump."

That night, an officious young Austrian officer asked to see everyone's papers. He strode into each compartment and demanded that Jewish passengers come forward. When he reached my father and saw the saxophone case, he grew suspicious. My father swore it was only a musical instrument, but the young officer was intent on showing his authority. "Open it at once!" When my father opened the case, there was nothing there but a shiny saxophone. The officer looked humiliated. Not to let the incident pass, he seized the instrument, lifted it over his head, and shook it. A large grapefruit hit him square in the face.

The passengers burst out laughing. Derisive laughter is not welcome to young Nazis. The officer had lost face to a Jew. He ordered my father into an empty compartment.

"I know you're lying," he shouted. "I know you're hiding something. Take off all your clothes. I'm going to search you."

My father started to undress, when the train suddenly began to slow down. The officer went to see what was happening; he was gone for only a minute, but that was enough. Recalling the conductor's warning, my father grabbed his clothes, leapt from the train, and started running for his life. When his friends in the compartment saw him, they opened the window and threw out his instruments. He gathered them up and, with his arms full, hurried away. Just then, a woman appeared on the road, pushing an empty baby carriage. If it happened in a movie you'd mutter, "How convenient." But there she was. My father loaded his instruments into the baby carriage, and the two walked off toward Liechtenstein. After checking into the Wald Hotel, he realized that he was a fugitive from the Austrian authorities. He sent word to my mother that he could never return to Vienna. She would have to join him in Liechtenstein, and then they must try to get to America.

The pressure grew on my mother to make a speedy exit. The old world was rapidly being replaced by an ugly new one. Two days later, my mother found herself on a list. The superintendent of her building had denounced her. This was very common in Vienna at that time. In a few months, a name on that list would have meant deportation to a concentration camp. But for now they just wanted my mother's apartment.

She was a resourceful, ingenious woman; she knew it would not be long before the Nazi collaborators came to her apartment to take anything valuable. All she had was the house money, and she was certain they would search in the usual places—under the mattress, in jars, drawers, and closets. So she unscrewed the light bulb in the bathroom fixture, stuffed the cash into the socket, and screwed the bulb back in place. On the day she was evicted, the superintendent searched the apartment. Then he searched the clothes my mother was wearing. Finding nothing, he ordered her to leave at once. All she was permitted to take was an overcoat. As she was being escorted to the street, she convinced him she had to go back and use the bathroom. So she returned to the apartment and, unblinking, headed straight for the bathroom, unscrewed the light bulb, and left with her money in her pocket.

My father soon made arrangements to get her out of Austria. She was smuggled out on the floor of a car, covered by overcoats. A few weeks later, my parents left Liechtenstein and were granted a temporary visa in Switzerland. My mother got a wonderful job there, working at a day-care center for children. She was born to be around children; she had a gift that made her caring and patient with them. Had they been permitted, my parents would have stayed in Switzerland, and I would have spent my days in a chocolate factory. With their permits expiring, they stood on still more interminable lines to emigrate to America. My mother had a brother, Ernst, in Chicago, and she yearned to be with him. My parents' route took them to Italy, and they finally sailed for the United States.

They landed at Ellis Island and disembarked on Thanksgiving Day, 1937. It wasn't for several days that they realized Americans do not eat turkey and cranberry sauce every day. My mother's original plan was to go straight to her brother's house in Chicago. But we also had a relative in New York, a man I came to call "my syrup uncle" because he had amassed a fortune selling sweet, fruit-flavored syrup. When my father told him of his plans to go to Chicago, my syrup uncle took him aside, shoved a ten-dollar bill in his pocket, and as God is my judge, anticipated my friend Fred Ebb by half a century by saying: "Max, stay in New York. If you can make it here, you'll make it anywhere."

So my parents became New Yorkers. It was hard to learn the new language and adjust to the fast pace and un*gemütlich* style of life here. Where were the courtly manners and the gentle music? My father could not fathom what he heard on the radio. Instead, he played only what he knew and was welcomed with open arms by a large group of displaced refugees. Certainly he was not going to grow rich doing this, but at least he would be able to play the Viennese music he loved.

My father was very talented, and had he been allowed to stay in his homeland, perhaps he would have been able to reach his true potential. Instead, he would have to live out his life, year after year, playing Viennese balls at the Waldorf-Astoria, performing at private parties, for those who adored the waltzes of Johann Strauss. Yet he could never really feel comfortable in America. He knew he was not stretching his musical horizons in New York, and perhaps that inner struggle led him to attach his thwarted hopes onto his son. But those aborted desires never left him, and I think they chewed at him all his life.

All my mother wanted, when they got here, was to start a family.

"There's no money, Lilly," he shouted. He was dead set against the idea. "*Bist du verrückt?*"

Verrückt or not, the unsinkable Lilly knew she'd find a way. Though it took her seven years to outsmart him in the bedchamber, Lilly Hamlisch victoriously gave birth to my sister, Theresa, always known to us as Terry. Not to say that he wasn't thrilled by his daughter, but more important, my father now felt he had fulfilled his obligation to my mother. That would be the end of it. No more children.

"Maxel," my mother would say, "when we die, we don't want Terry to be alone in the world. She needs a brother or a sister.

"*Bist du verrückt?*"

This time my father meant business. This time it was over his dead body. But he should have known better. He was no match for Lilly.

On September 2, 1943, a cool, breezy autumn evening, Lilly made one of her renowned dinners, a special treat to end all treats. As the smell of the *Kartoffelsuppe* made its way from the kitchen, my father sniffed the air and knew that he was about to partake in a meal he had not eaten since the glory days of the Hapsburgs. The cucumber salad had just the perfect blend of tart and sweet. The main course, his favorite, veal cutlets, was unbelievably succulent, almost sensuous. And that night, my mother brought the wedge of lemon to the table and hand-squeezed it for him, just as he loved her to do.

The dessert? From what I've heard, that was beyond even something that I can describe. The Sacher torte, *mit Schlag*, was a confection so perfect that words continue to fail me to this day. The candles flickered late into the night. By evening's end, Max reached toward his beloved and slowly whispered, "Lilly, you've done so much for me all these years, how can I ever repay you? Tell me, Lilly."

Exactly nine months to the day, Marvin Hamlisch was born. Thank you, Sacher torte *mit Schlag*.

3.

SIXTEEN AND GOING NOWHERE

By the time I had completed the sixth grade, I started going to Broadway shows by myself. I had already seen and loved *The Pajama Game*, *Damn Yankees*, and *West Side Story*. I still recall the thrill I got from hearing John Raitt sing "Hey There" into a dictaphone and then sing a duet with himself on the playback. It was such a theatrical moment. Seeing Gwen Verdon do "Whatever Lola Wants, Lola Gets" in *Damn Yankees* excited me, too, and hearing Larry Kert sing "Maria" made it clear that this was the world I wanted to live in. It was an era on Broadway that created its own magic. I'll never forget those Saturday matinees when I had squirreled away enough money for a standing-room ticket.

I was a good student at P.S. 9, and I was also doing well at Juilliard, getting good grades and maintaining my scholarship. But now it was time to enroll in a junior high school. Because I was going to Juilliard on Saturdays, taking piano lessons, practicing two hours a day now, and going to the theatre more and more, my parents thought I should attend a school that made minimum demands on my time. So my father began a search.

His goal was to find a school that gave me more time to prepare for my musical career. Typical of Max Hamlisch, he embarked on an intensive course of research. At the time, he was the onstage accordionist in a play starring Nehemiah Persoff. My father asked Persoff the same thing he asked everybody in those days: "What school do you think would be good for Marvin?" Persoff was a graduate of the Professional Children's School (PCS) and recommended it. After checking the school and assessing the alternatives, my father decided it was the place for me.

He little dreamed that in an effort to find a school that would free my days for the study of classical music, he would throw me into the lap of show business. Talk about your irony. The student body of PCS consisted of a handful of aspiring, serious musicians but mainly of kids with jobs on Broadway, in the movies, on television, in commercials, in modeling. These were youngsters making money, building careers in the entertainment business, and getting their education at the same time. Unbeknownst to my father, he was feeding my love of show business. He had put a rabbit in charge of the lettuce.

PCS was a "no frills" school. We spent a truncated school day that only extended from 10:00 A.M. to 2:00 P.M. Could anyone get a decent education that way? Apparently you could, because PCS graduates were admitted to many of the best colleges. The school managed its shortened school day by concentrating on academic subjects. There was no gym period, no home economics, no woodcraft. PCS was the place where, when you asked a fellow student how he was doing, he would answer: "Ask my agent." And into this breeding ground of show-business talent came Marvin Hamlisch, this gangly, prepubescent straight arrow, used to egg creams at the candy store with his uninitiated friends. Now I found myself with stacked, precocious, gorgeous girls and handsome boys who were in Broadway shows and in the movies. And when school was over, they went off to face a camera, or better still, an audience, while I went home to PRAAAACTICE!

The girls I had met at P.S. 9 were nice girls. The girls at PCS were flammable. They had faces that held a thousand promises and bodies that stood behind every one. These actresses, ballerinas, and professional models were heart-stoppingly beautiful. It was during a ballet sequence that was staged by some of my classmates that I developed a reverence for the leotard. (By the ninth grade it was more like an obsession.)

But there was a problem with all this exposure to beautiful faces and shapely bodies. I became preoccupied and dissatisfied with how I looked, and a complex took root at PCS that was to stay with me for a long time. I mean, Christopher Walken was a classmate of mine. Now you tell me: if a girl was going to ask one of us to a dance, which one would it be? Of course, if she needed a pianist to play while Christopher was making out with her, we might end up with a package deal. This complex was quite painful for me at the time, but my piano always came to the rescue. For when I played it, watch out—girls suddenly took an interest in me. I could compose a song on the spot using their names. (I had a little trouble with a girl named Ursula.) It was like a magical power, a musical aphrodisiac that I could invoke on command. Alone, I was likable, but with a piano, I was something special. If buses and cabs had pianos in them, many of my dates would have ended differently. Back then, I didn't mind that people liked me simply because I could play. I liked meeting all the kids who were working on Broadway, the place I realized more and more was the place I wanted to be.

I've always felt like something of an outsider. At Juilliard, I was awash in students of serious music, yet I loved Broadway show tunes. But I was never more an outsider than when

I arrived at PCS. I was still bringing my lunch to school in a paper bag, making sure I had enough carfare, and eking out an existence on a small weekly allowance. These kids were already rolling in dough, juggling schoolwork and high-flying careers. There was Leslie Uggams, with a great voice even then; there was Rex Thompson, who played Eddy Duchin's son, Peter, opposite Tyrone Power, in *The Eddy Duchin Story*; there was Josh White, Jr., son of the famous folk singer; there were actors who played the Asian kids in Rodgers and Hammerstein's *Flower Drum Song*.

If nothing else, PCS accelerated my appetite for musicals. I was finally meeting the kids who were out there *doing* it. The gap between my classical music lessons and my popular music leanings grew as wide as the Grand Canyon when I got involved with creating shows at PCS that featured these real-live professionals. This was my first taste of what show business was all about. I'm a seventh-grader, and the addiction to Broadway was already complete. There is no known withdrawal program for someone who is hooked on Broadway, not even unemployment.

The P.S. 9 production of *H.M.S. Pinafore* didn't compare with the professionalism of the shows at PCS. In my early days there, I had written one or two songs for their in-house revues. But by the time I reached the ninth grade, something wonderful happened. I met a young fellow named Bobby Mariano who had just entered the school and promptly became my best friend. Bobby was a dancer appearing on Broadway in *The Music Man*, and one day he said to me, "Why don't we create an original school show and stage it in a theatre?" Instantly, I found myself writing the entire score for a musical. This gave me the first chance to throw my composing talents into high gear. Thankfully, there weren't many composers in the school; the students were mainly performers. So when Bobby's idea surfaced for doing a full-fledged show using the talent of our students, there wasn't a lot of debate on the question, "Who'll write the score?"

The task of writing twelve to fifteen original songs did not intimidate me. Hell, it delighted me. I called Howard Liebling, and we started writing. It's hard to explain how we did what we did, but it hasn't changed a lot from those rosy days at PCS.

When I think about a song, I start with what it should say, what it should mean in the scene that it's in. I consider the purpose of the song before I think about the music. Once my lyricist gives me a title or once we agree on what the song is all about, I head for the piano and try to find the right "feel" for the song. Only then do I try out the melody. Though Hammerstein handed Rodgers all the words for a song and then Rodgers proceeded to write the music, I just can't compose that way. A full set of lyrics, without music, would constrain the rhythm of the song, and I find it hard to write a melody to a mandatory rhythm. I like to write the melody first. If the lyricist hands me the first few lines, that's enough. My brain can only take so much composing. I'm good for three or four hours at the piano at a stretch. Then I need a rest, or a sandwich. No, I don't sit in a garret with a wine bottle and a flickering candle. I know it worked for Beethoven, but not for me. Which is only fitting, since I'm no Beethoven.

Let me tell you about Bobby Mariano. Bobby was a Mickey Rooney surrogate. He talked like Mickey Rooney, had the energy of Mickey Rooney, and just as Mickey often had Judy Garland as his leading lady, Bobby was the real-life boyfriend of a girl who attended Scarsdale High. She was a talented, rambunctious kid named Liza Minnelli.

Bobby and I were a team. If we were the dynamic duo, we had a third fellow whom we both adored. His name was Lorin

Hollander, and by age fifteen he was considered one of the greatest pianists in the world. (He still is.) Even then he was concertizing and winning prizes. If I could have, I would have seen to it that Lorin had been my father's second son. Lorin was the essence of the classical musician. He used to come to our apartment to play the piano, and he'd dazzle everyone. My father would sit there, mesmerized by him, and I could tell he was wishing that I could play like that. I could tell that my father was thinking: "After all his Juilliard training, Marvin isn't really using his talent. Hollander is someone who is using his gifts properly." Ironically, Lorin was awed by my ability to write music. The reason our friendship flourished is that we had a mutual admiration: I envied him as a pianist; he envied me as a composer.

Lorin was used to playing on a Steinway grand; we had a Sohmer upright. When he played on our piano, he'd play with such gusto that, in addition to sending shock waves all the way to Amsterdam Avenue, he'd usually demolish a key or two. We'd wind up having the instrument repaired. Sometimes when he would drop by the apartment, I could see the look of distress on my mother's face; she was praying that he wouldn't play. "Oh, my God, if Lorin bangs on our piano, it's going to cost us another eighty dollars!"

When Bobby and I wrote and staged our big show, we turned to Lorin for his advice and ideas. You'll notice that even in my choice of friends I seemed to find myself in the middle—between Bobby and Lorin, between show business and serious music, between Shubert Alley and Carnegie Hall.

So Bobby and I set out to create a musical revue. It was 1960. We mounted it in a real theatre, the Little Carnegie, which normally served as a movie house and had an honest-to-God marquee. On opening night I had my first thrill of sitting in a theatre and hearing a voice inside me shout: "They're playing my song!" *All of Us*, as we called it, was a smash. If nothing else, it was my launching-pad experience. I may have been only fifteen, and the show had its faults for sure, but thinking about it now, there were real professional kids in the cast, the sets were first-rate by any standard, and if I must say so, I was on my way to writing some pretty good songs. I learned the fundamentals of show-song writing that are as valid now as they were then.

The chemistry between the composer and lyricist is key. If it's not there, bail out and get a new partner. A funny song that isn't funny is a disaster; it passes as quickly as gallstones. A ballad that lacks real emotion may be easy on the ears, but it doesn't move the soul and gets you nowhere. An "up" tune's got to jump. Otherwise, the audience jumps out of their seats and leaves the theatre.

Casting is critical. Hearing one's song sung beautifully is not the only aim in picking a singer. A song has to be sung in character. It's like asking Julie Andrews to do a number intended for Elaine Stritch. When a song doesn't work, it needs to be fixed. Fail to fix it, or refuse to fix it because you are on an "ego trip," and you lose a theatrical moment that might have been wonderful. But above all, don't ever underestimate an audience. No matter how terrific you think your song is, you really don't know how good it is until the houselights come down and the audience tells you. There are no instincts like the instincts of an audience.

All of Us ran for three glorious, sold-out nights. To this composer's way of thinking, I'd paid my dues and was ready for the Great White Way. But, of course, my schizoid life continued unabated. Monday through Friday I was immersed in school and homework. On Saturdays, I was playing Beethoven, continuing to struggle with the Juilliard curriculum and wearing the solemn look of a concert protégé. Although I gained some modest celebrity at PCS, I was never able to let the teachers at Juilliard know what I was up to. It was a frustrating feeling, because I knew beyond question that if they knew what I was up to, I'd be out on my "ear."

My friend Bobby was dating, as I said, that girl from Scarsdale named Liza Minnelli. I knew she was very talented even then, and it was obvious where her talent originated. There were no better vocal genes than Judy Garland's and no better theatrical genes than Vincent Minnelli's. Moreover, Liza had those incredible eyes and tons of enthusiasm. She talked fast, as fast as I did. (Barbra Streisand, when I first met her, said: "Do you know Liza Minnelli?" When I said I did, Barbra came back with "I knew it! You talk as fast as she does.") The three of us—Liza, Bobby, and I—shared some great times together.

It was Christmas of 1960 when Liza came up with an inspired idea for a gift for her mother. She wanted to record some original songs and give them to her. This was Liza's adroit way of telling her mom just how much she wanted to be in show business and to demonstrate that she had the stuff to be a great singer.

"Marvin," Bobby said, "why don't you and Howard write some songs for Liza?"

Howard and I promptly wrote them; Liza loved them and recorded the "demos" in a little studio, supported by piano, bass, and drums. Each one was specifically tailored to her: "The Travelin' Life" was big and brassy (she made it part of her first album when she turned professional); "If and When" was a tender ballad that displayed Liza's vulnerability; "Two Note Song" was a ditty that proved she could make you smile; and the last was a ballad called "So Many Dreams."

She was so excited with how the demo sounded that she

invited Bobby and me to her house for the Christmas party at which she would make the presentation to her mother. Obviously, this was no ordinary Christmas party for me, for I was going to meet the fabulous Judy Garland. Sixteen-year-old Marvin Hamlisch could hardly believe that he was about to meet the singer of his dreams. Most kids get lulled to sleep with "Lullabye and Good Night." But at my bedtime it was "The Trolley Song" and "You Made Me Love You." My only worry was that after meeting her, would there be anything more to live for?

By the time Bobby and I reached Liza's Scarsdale house that evening, forty or fifty people had arrived. I tried to present a cool, calm exterior, since, after all, I was already an accomplished composer with one high school production to my credit. But my composure deserted me the instant I entered the house. I mean, I came from a tiny apartment on the West Side of Manhattan. This place looked like the perfect setting for the signing of a peace treaty. The house even had a dining room. What the heck was a dining room? Greeting me at the door was none other than Judy herself.

There were waiters and butlers everywhere. No one had ever told me that hors d'oeuvres came *before* dinner. But my mother had told me to make sure I was polite, and so I said yes to every pig in a blanket and fried mozzarella stick as well as to every offer of caviar, liver pâté, cheese and toast, and smoked salmon. (At least this had some recognition factor: It looked like lox to me.) I was stuffed and wildly surprised when I heard: "Dinner is served."

After we'd finished, it was time to exchange Christmas gifts. Liza went over to her mother and handed her a beautifully wrapped package. She asked for quiet as her mother opened it. Judy seemed startled by it all. Liza took the record from her mother, and with a flourish, she set the record on the turntable. There wasn't a sound in the house. Then the music started, and a voice filled the room. It was a voice at once strange and familiar, young and confident, but with an eerie likeness of unmistakable heritage—mother and daughter.

At first, Judy didn't realize who was singing. But when she did, she actually wept. It was one of the most startling moments in her life. And I stood speechless, watching as the great Judy Garland looked on at her own daughter's debut—singing four of my songs.

Then Judy came over to me, thanked me for what I had done for Liza, and asked in that girlish voice of hers if Liza and I would do it again right there.

I went to the piano. Liza sang her heart out. It was even better than the demo.

But I was totally bowled over when Judy asked: "Wanna play for me, Marvin?"

I never thought I'd get to heaven before at sixteen, but I did. I played the piano as Judy Garland sang "The Trolley Song," "The Man That Got Away," "San Francisco," and "Somewhere Over the Rainbow."

If I could have phoned the world that night, I would have done it.

As the party wound down, Judy asked me if I'd like to spend the night. When I hastily accepted, Liza showed me to a guest room with a queen-sized bed with blue silk sheets and blue silk pillow cases. I was enthralled by the silk sheets and flabbergasted by the fact that I had my own room. There was a phone beside the bed, and I immediately used it.

"Hello, Mom? You're never going to believe this. They loved the record and then I played for Judy Garland and now I'm staying in the guest room and there are *blue silk sheets* on this really huge bed and *blue silk pillow cases* and I don't have to share this room with anybody." I had turned into a living run-on sentence.

When I told all this to my mother, I made a small confession: "I probably won't get under the covers because I don't think I could make this bed properly in the morning. I mean, there are top sheets and second sheets and sheets for the sheets . . ."

"Don't be silly, Marvin. Get under the covers."

"I don't think so," I said doubtfully. "I don't want Judy Garland to think I don't know how to make a bed."

So I slept on top of the covers with my overcoat as a blanket. It took me quite a while to fall asleep. I mean, why would anyone want to sleep on a night like this and give up feeling so good? Not only was this the first time I'd ever slept in a room alone; it was the first time I'd ever slept in a bed in which I could turn over without winding up on the floor.

Morning came: breakfast with Judy, Liza, her sister Lorna, and Bobby. It was astounding to me that not only were breakfast and dinner *not* served on the same table; they weren't even served in the same *room*. When it was time to leave, I asked if I could get a lift to the train station.

"The train station?" asked Miss Garland. I was sent home in a Cadillac limousine. The car was bigger than our living room.

As the driver turned into West Eighty-first Street, I worried that the Caddy might rebel at its alien surroundings. I mean, this was a Scarsdale limousine, and here it was in the grim, gritty city.

"Mom," I shouted as we pulled up to the curb. "Look out the window. It's me."

I raced upstairs. I couldn't wait to tell my parents all the details of my enchanted evening. I told them again about the fun, the food, the music, the people, the big bed, the blue silk sheets. When I was all talked out, my mother said rather enigmatically: "If something can give you so much pleasure, I never want it to change for you."

I didn't understand what she meant until that night when I went to bed. My mother had gone out and used her pocket money to buy me my own blue silk sheets.

If there was ever the slightest chance that I would forsake show business for the concert stage, it died on the night of the blue silk sheets. Now, more than ever, I knew where I belonged. I loved the people I was meeting, I loved the energy they generated, I loved the aura of excitement that surrounded them. I loved the craziness, too. I felt at home. My father would have to understand.

Oh, by the way. These days I prefer cotton wash-and-wear sheets. Fitted.

My Judy Garland limousine days were short-lived. I was back on the jam-packed Columbus Avenue bus on the way to school. My classmates were all building whirlwind careers and breezed in and out of class only when they were in New York to see their agents. Me, I hadn't missed a day. By now the euphoria of *All of Us* had subsided, and there I was sixteen—and unemployed.

I was told dozens of times at the Little Carnegie: "Marvin, you've got what it takes. Your songs are terrific, kid." But nothing was happening. I had already written a bagful of songs and had a three-inch pile of rejection letters. Music publishers were looking for rock songs, and I was writing music for Ethel Merman in *Gypsy*. The problem was that I never went through what normal teenagers do—most of my friends were dancing to rock; I never even learned to dance. But dance or no dance, like it or not, I would have to give them what they wanted. Nothing would contain me until the radio in the bathroom was blasting Marvin Hamlisch. I called up Howard: "Let's write like crazy this weekend. I'll even cut classes at Juilliard."

What began as a weekend of musical frenzy grew into months and months of turning out songs. We had "Pretty Penny," "Then You Came Along," "Easter Sunday," "At the Hop," "I Got Your Telephone Number from Johnny." On the optimism scale of one to ten, we were batting eleven. We were already counting the money. My father, on the other hand, was counting the hours I was spending away from practicing.

We went back to the recording studio and made demos, but this time we made up our minds to pound the pavements, door to door, and face up to these record guys. In the music business, there was one notorious landmark called the Brill Building, that legendary place where New York's music publishers supposedly conduct their business. You had to admire these people. In an office the size of a broom closet, with a pastrami sandwich in one hand and a bottle of Cel-Ray in the other, they always had time for little else but to tell composers they hated their music.

Solly Plotkin had no use for "Pretty Penny"; Harvey Schwartzfeld told me after hearing "Then You Came Along" to keep moving; Yossel Schmuel heard "Easter Sunday" and said: "This won't make it with the Catskill crowd, but come back when you got something for Passover." We came oh, so close with Vinny "DeBoss" Cinza, who listened to all of "I Got Your Telephone Number from Johnny" but then said: "Don't call me, I'll call you." After months of these turndowns, I found myself moving from obscurity to oblivion.

Howard and I, unfazed, went back to the drawing board. This time it took only two days to strike gold. Two Jewish boys came up with a novelty Christmas song: "What Did You Get Santa

Claus for Christmas?" This was no *Missa Solemnis*—but then, I'd never seen that one on the *Billboard* charts.

Having exhausted the first eight floors of the Brill Building, we started on nine. And there he was; the name on the door said BIENSTOCK. He had the clear, honest eyes of a used-car salesman and was puffing smoke in my face as he half-listened to the Christmas song demo. We were at the door and on our way out when the surprise came.

"Hey, kids, I like this 'present for Santa Claus' idea. You've got something here. I think I can do something with it."

This was it, and I knew it. A surefire smash. My name would be a household word in more than just my own household.

Mr. Bienstock told us he'd get back to us as soon as he had a deal with a singer. Each day when the phone rang, there was the inevitable pandemonium: "It could be Mr. Bienstock." Usually it was my Aunt Lolla. Or someone trying to sell us bossa nova lessons.

It must have been a week after Thanksgiving, 1960. The telephone rang.

"Lilly! Congratulations!"

"Congratulations for what?" asked my mother.

"Marvin's song—it's on the radio. Something about a present for Santa Claus."

My mother raced to tell me the good news. I flew to the radio, but I had missed it. I couldn't help wondering why I hadn't heard from Mr. Bienstock. I got it. He was so busy making stars out of unknowns that he just hadn't had time to get back to me.

Slowly, sadly, we learned about that fine line between plagiarism and coincidence. The truth was that the song Aunt Lolla had heard was not "What Did You Get Santa Claus for Christmas?" It was "Let's Give a Christmas Present to Santa Claus." Now, I guess it's possible that someone else could have had our idea at the exact same time we wrote our original song. I guess it's possible two songwriters could have coincidentally come up with the same idea simultaneously and used almost the same words to express them. The similarity may have been accidental. And maybe, as Nikita Khrushchev once said, someday shrimp will whistle. But being a Jewish mother, mine *knew* that her son's song had been "*gestohlen*." She knew with that marvelous instinct that all mothers possess that her son had been violated, exploited, abused. To give you some idea of how seriously my mother took the apparent theft of her Marvin's song, the stress and strain of the episode, as she consulted a battalion of copyright lawyers and friends, produced gallstones.

It was appropriate that the bodily part involved gall, because to my mother that was what Bienstock had plenty of. And my mother wasn't the only one in the Hamlisch household affected by the stolen-song saga. The commotion weighed heavily on my father. He was less concerned about who gave Santa a gift for Christmas than what his son was doing with his own gifts. My father was grappling with this fresh evidence that I was squandering my talent on a career in Tin Pan Alley. As for me, the whole experience was enough to shake my belief in Santa Claus. First the tooth fairy, now this.

I was devastated. I began to realize how vulnerable I was, how much I was at the mercy of the Bienstocks of the world. How much older would I have to get before success would be mine? Seventeen? Eighteen? But more important, this episode set off serious reflection. What kind of a musician did I want to be, anyway? Had I been seduced at too early an age by the world of pop charts? Commercial success could be tempting, but I had been insatiable. Had I misjudged my father and the real value of

Juilliard? I was much too young to have to sacrifice one musical gift for another. Then came a real breakthrough. I found that I could do many things; I could be as comfortable writing rock and roll as I could be writing show songs or playing Beethoven's Waldstein Sonata.

I began a kind of self-discovery, and odd as it may seem, I realized that my mind was like a cassette player. When the music needed to be important and serious, *click* . . . it was time to be the Juilliard pianist. If I was writing a rock and roll tune, *click* . . . "It's time for Marvin's music to be catchy, loud, driving." For the characters in our school show, *click* . . . . "expressive, tuneful, theatrical." I sometimes wonder why my mother never told me she'd given birth to a baby with a tape recorder in his head. It may not compare to *Rosemary's Baby*, but it's right up there.

I saw it all before me, laid out like a giant map. Not only was I going to stick it out at Juilliard, even if it killed me, but I was going to write the number 1 hit song before I was twenty-five, win an Oscar before I was thirty, and write the music for a smash Broadway show before I was thirty-five. Who was it who said, "Be careful what you wish for; you may get it"? Ring Lardner may have been right when he said, "The worst thing that can happen in life is to win a bet on a horse race at an early age."

I once read a short story by Somerset Maugham that made a nice analogy to the next important episode in my life. In the Maugham story, a guy gets fired from a menial job at a church when it's discovered he can't read or write. He thereupon creates a successful business that brings him wealth and happiness. Years later, a reporter learns of the tycoon's illiteracy and says, "Just think where you'd be today if you could read and write." And the guy says, "Yeah, I'd be back working at the church."

Howard and I had written a pop song called "Sunshine, Lollipops and Rainbows." Now comes a bit of serendipity. Quincy Jones, then head of Mercury Records, had an appointment to see his ear, nose, and throat doctor. The doctor was Lester Coleman, whom I had met at Judy Garland's party. He liked my music and had become a lobbyist for my talents. Doctors seem to like popular music. (Did you know there are more doctors writing popular songs than there are songwriters practicing medicine?) When Lester Coleman, ear, nose, and throat specialist to the stars, next had Quincy Jones in his office, he did a sixty-second pitch on my musical promise. How resistant can you be when your doctor has a swab stuck down your throat? Quincy agreed to meet with me.

A few weeks after he heard me play "Sunshine, Lollipops and Rainbows," he got Lesley Gore to record it. In less than two months, it shot to number 4 on the charts. Nothing could be better, not here on earth. The next weeks were heaven. I was shouting from the rooftops. There wasn't a radio station in town that wasn't playing it. All that Hamlisch misery wasn't for nothing. My plan was working; I had met the challenge and won.

Well, sort of. I mean, when the song was played on the radio, the disc jockey would say: "And here comes Lesley Gore's big hit. . . ." But, like Adlai Stevenson, I could have waited till hell freezes over before I'd ever hear him say: "And the music was written by that brilliant new composer, Marvin Hamlisch."

But never forget this. Call it the Jewish philosophy of happiness: There's a cloud behind every silver lining. Once a song has reached the apex of the *Billboard* charts, it plummets like a stool pigeon in the East River. It's depressing, all right. Let me sketch the chronology of a hit song. It takes about ten weeks for a record to reach the top of the charts. You get three short weeks of glory while it lives up there; then it drops. So you watch it go from number 4 to 13 to 33 to 56 to oblivion.

Howard and I struck again. After the success of "Sunshine, Lollipops and Rainbows" on the charts and in the profit-and-loss statement, we came up with a song called "California Nights." Like "Sunshine," it became another hit for Lesley Gore, riding to number 3. Sure, I knew these songs weren't exactly masterpieces, not even close. My father, though he couldn't honestly deny my achievement, was convinced more and more that I was just wasting my time. That's not how I saw it at all. Howard and I had had two songs on the charts, and there was money rolling in. Naturally, we quickly wrote a third song for her.

I arrived at the publisher's office knowing he was certain to be eager to hear the new song from his hot new team. I was ready for the royal treatment. Seated in his outer office, I waited for ten minutes. Then twenty. Then thirty. I read a dog-eared copy of *Cashbox*, thumbed through *Variety*, and glanced at *Billboard*, where my last song still nestled high on the list of moneymakers. Forty-five minutes. By now I was furious. When I was finally shown into his office, he had kept me waiting for a total of an hour and thirty minutes.

There was no apology. Not a grace note of explanation: "Well, kid, whaddaya got?" Maybe it was one-upmanship on his part. Maybe it was his constitutional lack of courtesy. Maybe it was my need for some recognition—after all, look what I had done for him. Whatever the reason, something inside of me snapped. No, I didn't kick him in the shin and hide in a suitcase.

"I've written two hits for you. I've made you a ton of money."

"That's true, Marvin."

"I won't be treated like this," I told him. "You know what I'm going to do with the song I brought you?"

And before he could say a word, I ripped it to shreds. I

scattered the sheet music on his carpet and marched out of the office.

As I rode down the Brill Building elevator, I felt as if I were caught in a trap. But was it of my own making?

Click . . . "You're writing down again, Marvin, trying to please everyone. For this you had to go to Juilliard?" Besides, this pop-music racket was taking an emotional and physical toll. I started getting stomachaches, bad ones. This could lead to ulcers. I could be stricken at the very moment when theatrical producer David Merrick walks into my life and begs me to write a show. I can hear him: "I would've loved you to do this, Marvin, but the doctors say we can't bring a baby grand into Mount Sinai."

That brings me back to the Somerset Maugham story. If Mr. Maugham were writing the story of my Tin Pan Alley days, he would conclude the tale with a reporter saying, "Wow, Marvin, just think where you'd be today if that song publisher hadn't kept you waiting for an hour and a half." And I'd reply: "Yeah, I'd still be writing pop tunes in the Brill Building."

Before I conclude this chapter, I'd like to tell you an incident in which my popular music, if nothing else, came very close to the ear of God. Every Friday night, as a child and stretching far into adulthood, my family and I went to services at the local temple two blocks from our apartment. Cole Porter was famous at Yale; Rodgers and Hart were renowned at Columbia. At my temple, Marvin Hamlisch was a name to conjure with. As you know, this was meaningful to my mother, because she wanted to hand down this tradition to my sister and me.

I was about seventeen years old, and I get a call at 8:30 A.M. one Saturday morning from my rabbi. That was somewhat unheard of for me. Not the caller but the hour. I didn't even know there *was* an 8:30 on Saturday morning. Anyhow, the rabbi says: "Marvin, you've got to help us. You've got to come and get us through the services this morning." (What kind of sermon did he want from me? The biblical meaning of a Lesley Gore hit?) Then he made himself clearer, which can sometimes be hard for a rabbi: "The organist is sick."

I promised to help out. But I had misgivings. Even though an organ and a piano are somewhat alike, there are differences that make an organ difficult for a pianist. For one thing, to sustain a note on the organ you have to hold the key down; on a piano you just depress the pedal. But I figured I could get away with it. Also, you must remember that for a typical morning service at our temple, there were maybe fifteen people in the congregation. Not exactly Sinatra at the Bowl. So who's going to know if I'm not at the top of my form? God might be watching if He's in the neighborhood, but I figure He'll be tolerant.

Fade up on the Mount Neboh Temple. Marvin sits astride the mighty organ, looking like a teenage phantom of the opera. Lilly, Max, and his sister, Terry, are seated up front, looking on with visible pride. (Didn't I once see this movie with Al Jolson?) I'm puzzling over which knobs to pull to make the organ loud or soft, vibrato or tremolo. I had my cues; I knew where the music was needed. The service began, and I was doing fine in the eyes of the Lord. Winston Churchill once said, "I am prepared to meet my Maker, but I'm not sure if He is ready for the confrontation." Well, Marvin was playing for his Maker. Whether or not his Maker was ready for Marvin is another question.

During the responsive reading, when rabbi and congregation read from alternate passages in the prayer book, no music was needed. I sat quietly and waited. Finally, we reached the moment for the "silent devotion." The rabbi had explained to me that the music for the silent devotion must be quiet, contemplative, intended to ease the soul. I fingered the keys in a solemn way. The music wafted through the temple, gentle, thoughtful, meditative.

Then I decided to make my mark. I've always tried to add something special to everything I do. Sometimes I get carried away. Not content with playing the bland, sonorous, nondescript music that the rabbi had requested, I tried to add the Hamlisch touch. As the congregation prayed and meditated, I went into a very somber rendition of "Sunshine, Lollipops and Rainbows." My father's chin dropped, my mother's eyes bulged.

The services finally ended, and the congregation headed for the street. As I reached the temple door, the rabbi stopped me. Uh-oh, time for the organist to pay the piper.

"Thank you for helping us, Marvin."

"An honor, Rabbi," I said.

"You really could do very well at this," he said.

"Thank you, Rabbi."

"Oh, about the music for the silent devotion."

Here it comes.

"I found it very inspirational, very inspiring."

4.

THE REHEARSAL PIANIST

"Sunshine, Lollipops and Rainbows" was one thing, but what I wanted desperately to write by now was the next great American musical. I was eighteen years old and *really* ready, but nobody was giving me the chance. I was standing on the sidelines, itching to enter the game. Isadora Duncan once said, "I danced in my mother's womb." If she could dance as a fetus, why couldn't I write a musical as a teenager? You may not believe this, but here's how I saw it back in 1962: how was it possible that not a single theatrical producer had the insight, vision, or courage to risk $800,000 on a brilliant, gifted, adolescent composer to write a Broadway musical? Alas, the injustice of it all. How many times since *All of Us* had I heard people say: "Marvin, if you're not headed for Broadway, nobody is." It seemed I'd have to lose my wunderkind status before anyone was smart enough to take me seriously.

At about this time, Liza Minnelli had gotten her first big break: She was starring in an off-Broadway musical called *Best Foot Forward*. It also starred Paula Wayne and Glenn (now Christopher) Walken. Her costar was a gifted young actor named Bob Dishy. And the person who was to become most relevant to me was the musical director, a fellow named Buster Davis.

Just as Dr. Coleman had lobbied for me with Quincy Jones, Liza was telling Buster about this gangly kid who was a Superman at the keyboard. One day, she insisted that Buster simply had to let me audition for him. I was a senior at Professional Children's School. You have to understand that you are still looking at a shy, straitlaced boy who wore a necktie to school. Every day, I'm surrounded by these laid-back kids, very cool, most probably smoking marijuana in the lunchroom while I'm munching a tuna fish sandwich.

Against this background, I suddenly get a phone call from Buster.

"Sweetheart, darling. Liza says you're terrific."

"Well, uh . . ."

"Listen, cutie, I'm looking for an assistant on a new show I'm working on. Come play for me on Tuesday at four. Let's do it at my apartment, sweetie. The show's called *Fade Out—Fade In*. You'll love it. We've got Carol Burnett, and the music's by Jule Styne" (my idol—the man who wrote the music for *Gypsy*). I had always loved Liza, and it's a rare friend (believe me, I know) who goes the extra mile.

Buster's apartment was on West Fifty-eighth Street. His dog was a basenji, a nonbarking dog. They make a noise, but they don't bark—sort of like a junior executive at Salomon Brothers. When Buster opened the door, he was wearing dark glasses. Indoors. To me this all seemed rather exotic.

"I can't wait to hear what you can do."

I had given a lot of thought to what I'd play for him. The piece of music I knew better than anything was the overture from *Gypsy*. When I was still in high school, one of my classmates was

Erik Lee Kirkland, the son of Gypsy Rose Lee. Through him, I had access to the best seats in the house for *Gypsy*. And God, did I use them. That show had it all: A brilliant score with lyrics by Stephen Sondheim, sparkling with gems like "Everything's Coming Up Roses," "You'll Never Get Away from Me," "Rose's Turn." And the incredible Ethel Merman.

"So, what are you going to play?"

"The overture from *Gypsy*," I say.

"Hit it," says Buster.

I proceed, pouring my heart into the score, playing my head off. When I was finished, the phone rang. Buster started talking, and it seemed as if there'd be no end to it. With the receiver still at his ear, he whispered: "Loved it, sweetie. Call you in a couple of days." I was sure I had played well, and, of course, I had a friend at court in Liza.

I was so confident, in fact, that I struck a deal with my father. The job was scheduled to begin in September. This coincided with my first semester at college. Grudgingly, my father agreed: I could take one semester off from Queens College if I gave him my solemn pledge to return to school—after I finished with the show—and get my degree. That was the deal. I grabbed it. I would have agreed to almost anything for a crack at Broadway. When you're stagestruck, any deal looks good. Remember the story about the actor who is dozing in his room when Satan appears and says: "I can make you a great star, but you'll have to forfeit your soul." And the actor says: "So what's the catch?" Well, I had my deal worked out with my father—but my catch was, I had no job. Two or three weeks went by, and I heard nothing. Not a whisper. I sensed myself getting depressed.

I must have blown it. Six weeks went by. Then eight. Where was Buster? I am usually able to spot opportunity when it knocks, and this job had opportunity written all over it. That's why I was so shaken. For a brief moment the door to Broadway had swung open, and now it had slammed shut.

I finally mustered the courage to phone him.

"What did I do wrong?" I asked. "Didn't you like my playing?"

"Marvin, you were fabulous," said Buster.

"So why don't I have the job?" I asked.

"Listen," he said. "The show's been postponed. Carol Burnett's pregnant."

"Pregnant!" I screamed. "Carol Burnett is pregnant, and that's why I'm not working on Broadway? How could she do that to me?"

"Sweetheart, don't take it personally. These things happen."

"Doesn't she know about the pill?"

Carol Burnett dares to get pregnant when my career is about to start.

"Marvin, the reason I didn't call you was Liza and I thought I should wait until I could line up something else for us. Listen, I have fabulous news. There's another Jule Styne show. There's a girl in it that is sensational. We'll be starting in three weeks. I need you to be my assistant."

I was dazed. I was trembling.

"Marvin, cutie, did you hear me? Are you still there?"

"I'm here, all right, Buster." By now the whole family had rushed to the phone wondering if I was going to faint. I whispered to my mother: "I got a job on a Broadway show."

By now, Buster was shouting into the receiver. "Marvin, are you sure you're all right?"

My mother whispered, "What's the name of the show?"

"By the way, what's the name of the show, Buster?"

"*Funny Girl*."

* * *

God took seven days to create the world; Buster needed just one phone call to create mine. The anticipation was unbearable as I waited for rehearsals to start. Finally, September arrived and rehearsals began. And thanks to Buster, I started to learn the way the Broadway world actually works. This was the real thing. This was working backstage. This was crummy rehearsal halls, up a flight of stairs to a barren room where the radiator is the coldest thing in the place. This was "Marvin, get me a cuppa coffee." This was an education in harmony, dialogue, and prune Danish. If I thought I knew what show business was all about before, I now knew I had a lot to learn.

I sat on the piano bench next to Buster as he played for rehearsals and taught the chorus the vocal arrangements as the score came to life. He was a damned good teacher. He wanted me to learn his job well enough so that I could replace him when the show went on the road for its out-of-town tryouts. At this point in Buster's life he took little pleasure in traveling.

Funny Girl was a musical about Fanny Brice, the classic clown of the Ziegfeld Follies. The star of our show was a relative newcomer named Barbra Streisand, who had come off a breathtaking performance in *I Can Get It for You Wholesale.* Critics said she had a stunning future, and they were right. Harold Arlen compared her to Beatrice Lillie, Helen Morgan, and the paintings of Modigliani.

In those days, Walter Cronkite used to host a show called *You Are There* in which the viewing audience felt they were present at certain moments in history that changed the world. The audience felt they were with Columbus when he discovered the New World or with some other legendary figure. Well, that's how I felt about Barbra Streisand. She was Christopher Columbus' New World of Broadway. I knew that Barbra would be the superstar she has since become. It didn't take a Juilliard-trained musician to know that this was the best voice anyone had heard in decades. She was destined to become a legend.

And, Mr. Cronkite, *I Was There*.

Barbra had her own rehearsal pianist, but on occasion I'd play for her. When I played for most singers, I was happy if the singer, song, and pianist created a professional sound. But it was much more than that with Streisand. I was a musician finding another musician who combined an original spirit with a voice that seemed like a sound from above. Her intonation was flawless, her interpretation impeccable, and when she held a note, it only got better. There was nothing she couldn't do with that voice, and she had an instinctual musical taste that brought genius to everything she sang. Goose bumps sprang up when I accompanied her on "People," and she proved that the right song and the right singer could create magic.

Of course, being a rehearsal pianist was just a pit stop in the big race to writing a show myself. Yet I soaked up everything that went on around me. I was eager to learn why certain things worked in a show and others didn't. Since the success of the show would hold no major consequences for the rehearsal pianist's career, I could watch the show's evolution without feeling the same degree of anxiety that the creators did. Nonetheless, I shared the agony and the ecstasy of getting a musical to work on Broadway.

My chief job was to write the notes for the background singers and chorus. If a principal actor sang the melody, the others onstage often acted as a backup group, singing the harmony notes. To me, of course, these were Marvin's and Buster's gems. That was a delusion. I was writing background vocals, while Jule Styne and Bob Merrill were making history and writing "People . . . people who need people . . ."

The out-of-town tryouts, as everybody knows, are the tense, draining days when scripts are rewritten, songs replaced, others tossed overboard, and show doctors imported to help out a show. I had heard the story of how playwright George S. Kaufman was once called in to save a musical that was in trouble on the road. It was being produced by an heir to the Bloomingdale fortune. Kaufman attended a performance in Boston, and the backer asked him for his advice. Kaufman said: "Close the show and keep the store open nights." Nobody ever advised producer Ray Stark to close *Funny Girl*. It had too much going for it.

For one thing, it had the story of Fanny Brice; for another, it had Barbra Streisand. Whether it's the talented clown who becomes a glamorous Broadway star or a flower girl who learns how to talk like a lady, the Cinderella story has always had a special appeal in the theatre. Of course, I felt as if I were living the Cinderella story myself: no more Gilbert and Sullivan at P.S. 9; no more musical revues at the Little Carnegie. *Funny Girl* was a blessing, and Buster Davis was nothing less than a saint. It is one thing to learn something in a classroom; it's another to experience it live.

For the first time, I found that my ability to play a song in any key on demand was proving invaluable. I could play anything in the score, anytime, anyplace, anywhere. Jule Styne would often sit down at the piano and run through some changes he wanted to make. These changes hadn't even been written down yet, but thanks to my good ear, I could instantly play back what I heard. With the plethora of changes that went into the show, that ability was a blue-chip commodity.

When I was not pounding the piano, rehearsing with stars, featured players, and chorus members, I was bouncing about as a junior underling, a gofer and man of all work. For example, Barbra Streisand loved those chocolate-covered doughnuts from Horn & Hardart. I was the guy who would race around the corner and get them for her. If you are ever playing Trivial

Pursuit and someone asks you: "What composer used to fetch doughnuts for Barbra Streisand?" you'll know.

Yet despite our optimism, the show that had looked so promising in rehearsal ran into problems. Scenes felt longish. The script lacked immediacy, and the whispers started: "We need more Barbra." It was like saying: "Just give the ball to Michael Jordan." Some of the songs didn't work. We were so mesmerized by Barbra's voice that we hardly noticed that some of them weren't serving the story.

Jule Styne and Bob Merrill struggled to rewrite the score. "Marvin, let's try this one."

"Marvin, we've got another one."

"Marvin, Marvin."

And so it went. I must have been fed brand-new songs every week. It was exhausting, but it was the best learning experience I could ever have asked for. I was finding the critical distinction between what makes a theatre song work and what doesn't. Jule and Bob wrote enough songs to score three shows and an operetta. Isobel Lennart, the librettist, kept fixing the book, and the cast kept learning and relearning dialogue and songs. All the while, Marvin, eyes and ears wide open, kept taking it all in.

By the time *Funny Girl* went out of town we were much more cocky and secure. The audience at the opening in Boston at the Shubert Theatre went wild for Streisand, but then one of the strangest things that I could have ever imagined happened during the second act. It seemed as if something suddenly triggered disapproval in a way that bordered on rebellion. People started leaving in droves. I don't mean a few people. I mean an entire audience, orchestra and balcony. It was as if word were spreading of a bomb threat. I've subsequently seen people walk out of shows, but never in such daunting numbers and never at the same time. When Barbra sang about people needing people, she could have been referring to our cast.

Were we sitting on a disaster?

Why were they leaving? What had we done to lose an entire audience? Immediately, there was a summit meeting of the minds. Garson Kanin, who was directing, Jule, Bob, Isobel, and me (in case someone wanted a pastrami on rye) all agonized over how to solve this puzzle. Everybody had an idea; everybody had an opinion. By 3:00 A.M., with nothing much accomplished, it was decided to meet again at the theatre in six hours.

Mysteries are often solved in odd ways. There they were, at 9:00 A.M., some of the greats of the theatre, all agonizing over what was causing this mass exodus. And they were coming up empty, which is rare for people with so much experience. Suddenly, there was the noise of a vacuum cleaner; the cleaning woman had started her day's work. She'd been vacuuming the Shubert for over twenty-five years, and she had seen hundreds of shows come and go. She made her way to the front of the house.

"Excuse me, Mr. Kanin. I'm sorry to interrupt."

She leaned over and whispered something to him.

Suddenly, there was excitement in front of the theatre. Garson turned to Jule: "This woman has something here. I think she's got it."

And then Garson spilled the beans. The cleaning lady had made it clear to him that we had unwittingly broken the golden rule of Boston theatre. We had to get the curtain down, she said, *before* they shut down the transit system. *Funny Girl* was so long, it was stretching to almost four hours, and the last train was at 11:45. We were good, but not good enough to rob people of their eight hours' sleep.

Looking back, that transit disaster was a blessing in disguise. Normally, when a show runs long, it gets nibbled away, a little each night, a few minutes at a time. Our battle with the Boston subway system resulted in the fastest, biggest cuts in show-business history. A full twenty minutes were lopped off before the mad dash to the trains began the following evening.

Now that we had everybody home on time, I thought it would be clear sailing from here on in. I knew there were some loose ends to tie together, but essentially I thought we were on the money. But remember—I've said it before—never take an audience for granted. They still adored Streisand, but they wanted the great story of the tragedies and triumphs of Fanny Brice, and the script still wasn't giving it to them. The Boston critics agreed.

Again more frantic meetings, more changes to be made. I saw how getting to Broadway could be so painful, with so many sleepless nights, tons of extra rehearsals, dozens of shouting matches, and a basketful of battered egos. While the cast rehearsed during the morning and afternoon, Jule, Bob, and Isobel rewrote and rewrote. These sessions went on for hours into the night.

I was poised at the telephone in my hotel room. Once Jule gave me the word, I would head for his room and collect the fruits of his night's labor. He asked me to transcribe the tape of the new material and rehearse with the cast. I closeted myself away for hours, and each time I hoped that these new songs would be the answer to our prayers.

Well, sometimes that was true. But lots of times one remedy didn't do the trick, and the audience was quick to let you know. I'd hear the coughing begin. No, not one or two people with a polite cough, but a lot of people with the croup. In the theatre, this is not a sign of an inflamed larynx. It means they've tuned you out. It was sudden death for me to hear them hacking away; some nights I thought of opening a concession stand in the lobby to sell Smith Brothers cough drops. Larry Gelbart, the creator of *City of Angels* and *A Funny Thing Happened on the Way to the Forum*, once said: "If Hitler is alive, I hope he's on the road with a musical."

Although the script was getting better, the one thing that never changed was the raves for Barbra Streisand. I remember how, at the beginning, I was overwhelmed by her, tremendously in awe of her. I never took my eyes off her. I developed a deep, dark secret about her. I couldn't dare tell her, or anyone else for that matter. But I started nurturing a dream, and I became obsessed with it. Every night I would say a prayer about it: "Please, God, one day, let Barbra Streisand sing one of *my* songs."

One of the new songs, "Sadie, Sadie, Married Lady," worked remarkably well. It was an anthem to Jewish brides, sung by Fanny and the chorus. From one night to the next, Barbra was given to changing the melody here or there. Jule Styne had allowed her that latitude, but when she did this, it threw the chorus out of whack. (Hey, wait a minute, that was my turf.)

One evening after the show, I got up my courage and went to see Barbra in her dressing room. I may have overstepped my bounds here, but I couldn't help telling her that by altering the song, she was throwing off the music of the chorus.

Barbra looked at me as though she had just landed on Plymouth Rock and I had just crawled out from under it.

"Marvin," she said, "what are these people paying money to hear—your vocal arrangements?"

The next night, I changed the background music.

And do you know something? She was absolutely right. Another vital lesson I learned quickly was that in show business the most rigid rule is to know when to bend.

Another rule is, when in trouble, if you can, get yourself Jerome Robbins, the great director and choreographer. He was a good friend of Jule's and was brought in to help. Methodically, Jerome Robbins went about making changes, and his instincts seemed infallible. In a few short weeks, he had pulled the whole show together. It was finally "frozen" and would stay that way.

My work was completed. What I didn't realize at the time was that once a show is frozen, people who are not essential to the production are let go. Nothing personal; it's just business. The producers do it to cut costs. Once the final vocal arrangements are learned, there's really no need to keep paying the arranger. It just naturally follows. Like election year and tax cuts.

We were about two weeks away from opening night on Broadway when I received a phone call from the company manager: "Marvin," he said with the sympathetic tone of a tax auditor, "your services are no longer required. You can go home."

I was devastated and demoralized. *Funny Girl* had been my family for these many months, and now I was dismissed. Fired. I had given my all through the tough times and the madness, and now that they had what they wanted, it was, it seemed to me, Screw loyalty; get lost, Marvin. The letdown was unbearable. Sure, I had prepared myself to leave after opening night in New York, but to be fired in Boston—and by the company manager no less—this was too much. "Thanks a lot and out with the garbage." I couldn't believe I wasn't going to be allowed to see this thing through, to enjoy opening night, the party, the reviews, the whole enchilada. To me it seemed like a personal affront.

I started to cry. The dream of being there on opening night had just gone down in flames. I'd never been fired before. I began packing my suitcase and began saying to myself: "I'm a failure."

I telephoned Buster and told him the news. I was hysterical. He tried to calm me down, to explain the facts of life in the theatre, but he didn't have much luck. I was screaming frantically:

"Buster, I can't believe it."

"Sweetheart, I know, I know—"

"I mean, really, I didn't make any mistakes. I broke my ass. I played more songs in more keys than anybody. I've hardly slept since I got to Boston."

"I know, I know—"

"You don't understand. I've been killing myself."

"Sweetheart, please—"

"Buster, what the hell am I going to do? I have to get out of here."

"Marvin. Stay there. I'll call you right back."

Ten minutes later, Jule Styne phoned my hotel room. "Marvin, come over to my office tomorrow morning."

I had been rehired. It was only years later that I understood how generous this was. There had been no reason on earth to put me back on the payroll. But Jule Styne and Buster Davis went to bat for me with the front office. They literally invented jobs for me, because they came to understand what all this meant to me, and they didn't want to see a dream die. Jule Styne had always treated me like a son. He let me learn so much from just watching him do what he does best—write music for the theatre.

Funny Girl opened at the Winter Garden on March 26, 1964. The moment the curtain came down, I ran backstage, into the middle of that special elation and euphoria that reign when there's no doubt in anyone's mind that you have a hit. This was pure mayhem, and I felt ecstatic to have been a part of it. I had taken my mother with me and I brought her backstage.

When we walked out the stage door, there were hundreds of people waiting for Barbra to appear. As I stood in the doorway with that joyous, expectant throng at my feet, I turned to my mother and said, "You see, Mom? You see what they think of the rehearsal pianist?"

Of course, no one was paying any attention to me, but a voice inside was whispering: "I love this!"

Buster Davis couldn't have been kinder or a more talented mentor. He had started it all. And from the beginning he knew he had an assistant who wanted to emulate him but would never push him aside. I was always there to defend him and make sure his arrangements would be performed faithfully. To this day, I can still say that Buster was the best accompanist I had ever seen.

Facing the harsh reality that *Funny Girl* was behind me, I now had Queens College peering over my shoulder. The promise to my father loomed as a major factor in my life. I had assured him that I'd return to school, and I was not going to go back on my word. To be honest, I wasn't quite sure why. If college is supposed to prepare you for the needs of the real world, why did I need any more preparation? I was getting well educated in the real world of the theatre. In fact, college just looked like an obstacle on the road to success. All too suddenly I was back there, treading the halls, doing homework instead of vocal arrangements, reading textbooks instead of *Playbills*.

But I had tasted the golden apple, and my appetite for another bite was voracious. The situation got even more complicated when Buster told me he was about to replace his assistant on *The Bell Telephone Hour*, the TV show for which he was the vocal arranger. He offered me that prized position as I was taking my finals in German 101 and Statistics. *The Bell Telephone Hour* was a musical jewel, with four or five guests on each show—everyone from Broadway stars to opera divas. Here my Juilliard skills would prove invaluable.

But how was I going to juggle my college schedule to let me work full-time on a TV musical spectacle? Impossible. Was there a chance that I could renegotiate with my father? Not a prayer.

There's a saying that some people actually believe. It goes: "You can't be in two places at the same time." To which I say: "Wanna bet?"

Rehearsals for *The Bell Telephone Hour* took place in New York. They ran from 10:00 A.M. to 5:30 P.M. for ten days straight. The show was broadcast "live"; then there were three days off. I was caught in the Queens College bind again. There was no way I would be able to meet their schedule of classes and do this show. I needed a solution. I assembled all the catalogues of the colleges in New York and discovered that a combination of courses at Queens, Hofstra, and the RCA School of Television would do the trick.

I'd leave home at 7:30 each morning to make an 8:30 class at Queens College. I'd get out of class at 9:30, jump in a cab, and reach Manhattan by 10:15 to take up my duties on the show. By 6:00 P.M. on Mondays and Thursdays I'd race out to Hofstra in Hempstead, Long Island, to take some other courses. By 6:00 P.M. on Tuesdays and Fridays I'd be in a classroom at the RCA School of Television, which gave me six more credits. At night, I'd do homework and write out music for the next day's rehearsal. As you can see, I've long believed that the greatest sin is sitting on your ass (unless it's in a cab, in a class, or at a piano).

All work and no play produced some uncomfortable side

effects. Because of my relentless pace, sometimes I started to get these terrific bellyaches. Usually they came and went quickly, but sometimes, particularly when I had skipped a meal or wolfed one down, they became quite severe. After a few months of suffering in silence, I saw a doctor. He suggested antacids. Soon I became a walking pharmacy; I could tell you the comparative efficacy of liquid Mylanta, chewable Maalox, Gelusil, you name it. I was working hard, going to sleep nightly at 3:00 A.M., and generally burning the candle at all three ends. (What? A candle only has two ends? Now you tell me.)

If you hadn't guessed by now, I made no friends at school. Who even had the time to say hello? With a cab waiting to whisk me off the campus, there was no time for pleasantries. But I wouldn't have had it any other way. The *Telephone Hour* gave me the chance to work with the likes of Lena Horne, Peggy Lee, Erroll Garner, Duke Ellington, Maurice Chevalier, Bing Crosby, and Leontyne Price. I was exposed to virtually every kind of music, from jazz to folk to symphonic.

Let me tell you about the logistics of the *Bell Hour*: Buster would prepare the music and meet with that week's guest stars to make sure all was well and the music was just right. He'd also arrange all the choir parts. Buster would do the arrangements at his apartment on West Fifty-eighth Street, and early in the morning, before class, I'd stop by. We'd discuss the music for the upcoming show; he'd tell me what he wanted, and I'd write it out and teach it to our guest stars. It was a heady routine. As far as my ability to arrange music for vocalists and copy it quickly, I can only say: *Funny Girl* made me the fastest pencil in town.

The music on the show was always high-level. I loved the songs, even though they tended to be old-fashioned. As I played them, week after week, I began thinking: isn't it time we started playing something new? I thought to myself: why don't we try just one of *my* songs on the show? I had a drawer full. Fat chance. This show concentrated heavily on the classics of yesterday.

The show held one other major frustration for me. It was embodied in the orchestral conductor, a man named Donald Voorhees. He was a big man, rigid in his walk and his manner. He never seemed friendly, except to the stars. He was at best a competent conductor, but he had an ironclad contract that secured his position until the northern ice cap reached Times Square. Sort of like a rabbi emeritus or a U.S. congressman. They're there till they drop.

While Buster was figuring out the arrangements, I rehearsed them every day for ten days. Voorhees would appear only for the last day or two of rehearsal. In a sort of ritual, I would hand him the stack of musical arrangements. It looked like the manuscript of *War and Peace* and weighed about twelve pounds. After he took possession of the music and had time to study it, I never heard a syllable from him about how good an arrangement sounded or how well a number worked. He'd only point out the one or two small errors. I felt like Mozart when the duke tells him, "There are simply too many notes." I decided that if ever Voorhees and I fought a duel and I had the choice of weapons, I would choose courtesy.

To put it mildly, Donald Voorhees and I never really hit it off. One reason for our lack of empathy was that he seemed somehow an outsider who would occasionally deign to enter our shabby rehearsal hall, glance at what we were doing, conduct the orchestra, and return to some distant celestial sphere of his own.

I must admit that I came to *The Bell Telephone Hour* as I had come to *Funny Girl*, an unabashed square. I still didn't drink or smoke or do drugs or work on the Jewish holidays. For me, those days are as clear a signal of the obligations of season as the Fourth of July and Christmas. When the High Holidays approached, I respectfully informed Voorhees that I would not work on those days. I didn't think it would prove a formidable problem to get another pianist for that short period. In fact, I knew of an able substitute. But Donald said: "No, Marvin, if you don't show up for work on the High Holidays, you're fired." I was stunned. "I don't want another pianist to show up here that the singers won't be used to. Make up your mind—if you take off the holidays, don't bother to come back."

I faced a crisis, one of principle. Could I work on Yom Kippur and violate something that was dear to me and would deeply offend my parents? Or would I lose a job that brought me income and a future in music? I remembered what Woody Allen had said at a pivotal time in his own career: "I faced a crossroads. One way led to despair and utter hopelessness, the other to total extinction. I prayed that I had the wisdom to choose correctly."

"Mr. Voorhees," I said, "if I work on the High Holidays, I will be fired from my *home*. There's no contest."

Voorhees didn't care about my problem. His indifference brought to mind what George S. Kaufman said to Eddie Fisher when the singer told him he was having a problem dating girls because of his youth. "Mr. Fisher," said Kaufman, "on Mount Wilson there is a telescope that can magnify the most distant stars. This remarkable instrument was unsurpassed in the world of astronomy until the construction of the Mount Palomar telescope, an even more remarkable instrument of magnification. Mr. Fisher, if you could somehow put the Mount Wilson telescope *inside* the Mount Palomar telescope, you *still* wouldn't be able to detect my interest in your problem."

I think George S. Kaufman would have understood my dilemma, but Donald Voorhees didn't, and there was nothing I could do to change his mind. With some people, the less you have to do with them, the less worse off you are. But Voorhees wielded a lot of power. He was forcing me to choose between my job and my beliefs. And I made my choice. As the High Holidays approached, I knew I would not show up for work. I figured the job was history.

Recalling the time I had been banished from *Funny Girl*, and Buster Davis had proved my guardian angel, I told him of my latest impending doom.

"That's just the way Voorhees is," said Buster. "He likes to make things difficult. He's actually not an evil guy. He's very good to his inferiors."

"But what do I do now?" I asked.

"Just stay away from him and talk to Barry."

I went to Barry Wood, the show's executive producer.

"I know that Donald Voorhees wants me fired," I told him. "But I just want you to know that I'm not coming to work on Yom Kippur. It's unfair."

"Can you get us a competent substitute to take your place?" Barry asked. "And I'd want you to go over the songs with him so he'd blend in."

"Sure," I said.

"In that case," Barry said, "enjoy your Yom Kippur. And send my best to your family."

In retrospect, maybe it would have been better to have been fired over the Yom Kippur caper. I was going into my third season with *The Bell Telephone Hour*, and I had done about as much as I could do. What kept me loyal to this assignment was Buster. Aside from that, I only kept doing it for the money. Between my salary and my copyist fees, I was making over $1,500 every ten days. Since I was still living at home with my parents, I had nothing to do with the money but put it in the bank. I eventually used my savings to help buy us a small summer house on Long Island.

But I was being driven up the wall. It became clearer to me, week after week, that I could not continue as a rehearsal pianist much longer. Fun with Buster was one thing, but there were tunes of my own constantly coming into my head. They had to find a place to be born. The TV job plus the demands of a full college program left me little time to compose. There was no time to give to anything except *The Telephone Hour*, school, and sleep.

My composing life was in hibernation. I was lying safe in the harbor when I should have been sailing. Where was this leading? *Carpe diem*, seize the day, said the poet. It was time to write music and let the chips fall where they may. I should have known that nobody ever stole second base while keeping his foot on first. What was happening to me? The Marvin Hamlisch who had them standing in the aisles at the Little Carnegie? What had become of the dream of the phone ringing and the voice telling me: "Marvin, I want you to do a show"? But how could the phone ring while I was tied up with Bell Telephone?

It would be nice to tell you that I stormed into the producer's office and bellowed, "That's it. I've had enough. I am leaving to make my name as a composer. Farewell, comrades." I suppose it's natural to want your life to read better than it was lived. But that was not the case. I never did anything: the decision was made easy for me: *The Bell Telephone Hour* went off the air.

A little breathing space opened in my life. And we know how nature abhors a vacuum. I was like a rookie who had made it to the majors, and each day I grew more confident, more impatient. I wanted my own turn at bat. I was ready to write my own

Gypsy. Like Rose, I wanted to shout: "Gangway, world, get off of my runway."

It was time to make my own music again. . . .

Being free of the *Telephone Hour* also meant that I had time to see what others were doing. I remember the day in 1966 when I was invited to see a run-through of a new musical and was free enough to accept. It was called *A Joyful Noise*. When it ended, I went over to the stage manager and asked him where the choreographer was.

"He's that dark-haired guy over there."

I walked over to him and said: "You don't know me, but I'm telling you, you're a genius. You may not believe this, but someday I'm going to work with you. I'm writing your name in my address book under 'G' for genius."

He was aghast. He took me in with his eyes.

"What's your name?" he asked.

"Marvin Hamlisch. What's yours?"

"Michael Bennett."

5.

THE SWIMMER AND THE HIT MAN

It felt strange going to college without dashing back to rehearsals. "Hmm, so this is the way most kids go to school? Interesting. They just concentrate on their studies. That should be a cinch." Frankly, I now felt I had too much free time. I had become accustomed to a hectic schedule. Like the seamstresses in *The Pajama Game*, I was used to racing with the clock. But now the hands moved more slowly. I was to stick to my vow: I would not take a job unless it was as a composer. So this was the first time since I was seventeen that I wasn't earning my way.

But the nice thing about this quiescent period was that my stomachaches had disappeared. Without having to juggle college and work, campus and television, I slowed down considerably. Mind you, I still had my old worn-out dream that the phone would ring and a voice would say: "Marvin, I'd like you to write a Broadway show despite the fact that you've only had two bubblegum hits to your name." Naturally, it didn't come true.

Then, out of the blue, a different kind of telephone call came. Ah, yes, I remember it well. It was a Saturday evening in 1967. It was around six-thirty. It was a woman with a voice brittle with impatience. She announced she had gotten my number from one of the musicians in *Funny Girl*, and that they needed a piano player for a party that night. She asked if I was available.

"Lady, please!" I said, affronted. "I'm a college student. I'm a Juilliard man. I was the rehearsal pianist for Barbra Streisand. I've worked on *The Bell Telephone Hour*. I'm a composer. I do not play parties. *Repeat, I do not play parties*."

"That's too bad," she said. "It's for Sam Spiegel."

"I'll be there in twenty minutes," I said.

How quickly the vows of a serious composer-in-the-wings flew out the window. But Sam Spiegel was the producer of *Lawrence of Arabia*, *On the Waterfront*, and other such blockbusters. Now I ask you, with what you know about me, was there any way I wouldn't show up for this? Grabbing my trusty tuxedo and making sure there were no bits of toilet paper on my freshly shaved face, I raced from the house and arrived at Sam Spiegel's suite at the St. Moritz Hotel.

As I began my four hours at the keyboard, I watched the place fill up with show-business notables. I felt a little like Moss Hart descending into George S. Kaufman's living room to find himself in the company of Alexander Woolcott and Dorothy Parker. Harold Rome arrived, and I quickly played a medley of his songs from *Wish You Were Here*; Betty Comden and Adolph Green appeared, and I went into a medley of their songs from *On the Town* and *Bells Are Ringing*. Faye Dunaway arrived amid a group of the 'A' List from Hollywood. Even Bobby Kennedy, who was running for a seat in the U.S. Senate from New York, made an appearance. I got the feeling that by being around these kind of people, something might lead to something—call it the blessings of propinquity. Branch Rickey said that luck is the residue of design. That's what a lot of opportunity is all about. If you create an atmosphere in which something unexpected may happen, often it does. I didn't want to find myself in the despairing position of the pug in Sam Spiegel's movie, complaining: "I coulda been a contender."

I sensed that Sam Spiegel was very happy that night. He was using a live piano player for the first time—he always used to play records—and he could see how much his guests were enjoying themselves. The thing about Spiegel was that he was built on the scale of one of his movies, a big, hefty guy, with a cigar jutting from his mouth like a gun barrel. He was from Vienna, and I let him know we had that common lineage. (No, I didn't play any Strauss.) When the party ended, he said he wanted to talk. Some of the guests, like Jule Styne, told Spiegel I was a talented young fellow. "What do you do besides play for parties?" he asked.

"Well, Mr. Spiegel, if this hadn't been your party, I wouldn't have taken the job. I am a . . . a composer."

Spiegel proudly told me that he had given Leonard Bernstein his big break when he hired him to write the score for *On the Waterfront*. I guess you could also say that Sam Spiegel had given Lawrence of Arabia his big break.

"I've got a new picture, Marvin," Spiegel continued, "and I'm looking for somebody to do the music. Tell you what. I'd love to hear a couple of your songs. I'll phone you in a few days. Then you can come over and play them for me."

Spiegel stuck a copy in my coat pocket of the John Cheever short story on which the film was based. It was called *The Swimmer*, and it was to star Burt Lancaster as an aging Lothario who decides one day to swim home, pool by pool. (Why he didn't just grab a cab, I've never understood.)

The one thing I did understand was that my mélange of songs—the top forty that nobody wanted to publish and my two big hits, "Sunshine, Lollipops and Rainbows" and "California Nights"—was not the most persuasive argument for my admission to the world of movie scoring. Particularly in a Sam Spiegel production. So I decided that before I met with Spiegel, I would have the main theme for the score for *The Swimmer* ready to go. I hoped it would reflect Cheever's brooding tone. A few days later, Spiegel called. I appeared at his hotel and announced grandly that I was not going to play any of my old songs for him. He was taken aback.

"What do you mean? You said you were a composer. So play me some songs."

"Mr. Spiegel," I said, "I'm not here to play you some songs. I'm here to play you the theme from *The Swimmer*."

I thereupon sat down at the piano and played what I'd written. When I finished, he said: "Play it again, kid." When I finished playing it a second time, Spiegel grabbed the phone and began calling a succession of people to come to the hotel to hear what I had done. He loved it. Over the next few hours I must have played it at least fifteen times.

"If this gets played on the radio as many times as I've played it today," I said, "we'll have a hit."

When the last listener had come and gone, Spiegel confronted me.

"Okay, that's it. I want you to do the movie."

"I'm ready," I said. "No problem." (I started wondering about college courses in California.)

Then Spiegel frowned.

"But can you *do* a picture? Do you know what it takes to score a movie?"

I looked him straight in the eye.

"Sure I do," I said.

The truth was that I didn't know the first thing about the movie business. I knew nothing about 35-mm film or click tracks or all the thousand and one things you have to know to write music for a feature film. I confess that I must have been given an uncanny instinct, and that was to know when an opportunity was at my door or when an offer came that could become a turning point. It never occurred to me, not even for a split second, to say to Spiegel that all this was brand-new to me or that I'd need a long course of study. I've always had the kind of chutzpah that lets me say: Give me the job and I'll figure it out later. My mother used to call this "making your own luck." Others call this "earn while you learn."

I had never thought about writing for films, but here was my chance to compose professionally, even if it was not yet for Broadway. Someone was going to pay me to write music. If this were a conventional success story, I would have been swept to Hollywood on the wings of song and a lucrative contract. If this were a movie, the scene would fade out on the gruff producer embracing the neophyte composer or the composer kissing his girlfriend as the music swelled and the end credits rolled. But that's not the way it happens in the real-live movie business.

In the real world, you hire a lawyer, and he gets in touch with the producer's lawyer, who makes you a ridiculous offer. Now Sam Spiegel had a reputation of being tight with a buck. (He made Jack Benny look like a philanthropist.) On the other hand, I realized he was taking a hell of a gamble on me. So I was ready to accept almost anything.

He offered me $2,500.

I knew that in those days, composers were getting anywhere from $25,000 to $70,000 to do movie scores. So $2,500 was definitely on the low side. Don't get me wrong. I knew opportunity was knocking. Still, it seemed unfair to write sixty minutes of music for eighty-five musicians for a multi-million-dollar movie for $2,500. You'd pay that for a refrigerator with an ice maker.

Mind you, I have read horror stories about artists whose sense of fairness fouled up their careers. Such as Charles Grodin telling how Mike Nichols offered him $500 a week to star in *The Graduate*. While Grodin was trying to negotiate a few dollars more, Nichols ran across another unknown named Dustin Hoffman. The director broke off negotiations with Grodin, who then had to wait another five years before getting his break in *The Heartbreak Kid*. Five years of kicking himself in the butt.

It was a very tough call. I wanted the job badly, and I knew this break wasn't going to come again soon. But I didn't want someone to take advantage of me. I decided to ask Quincy Jones. He had helped me out before. By now, Quincy was making a name for himself in Hollywood as a composer of film scores, including *The Pawnbroker* and *In The Heat of the Night*. I laid out the deal to him and confessed: "I don't know what the hell I'm doing. It seems like a lot of work for that amount of money. After all, I made fifteen hundred a week as a rehearsal pianist for *The Telephone Hour*."

"You're right, Marvin. You can't accept that," Quincy said. "Tell Spiegel to forget it. Walk."

"Walk?" I said.

"It's slave labor."

I reflected that Sam Spiegel must have learned a lot about slave labor from his film *The Bridge on the River Kwai*. I mean, nobody paid those prisoners a cent to build a bridge and whistle at the same time.

I decided to have my lawyer say I wanted more money. All during the negotiations I felt tense. I couldn't sleep for nights. You make a decision, and then other people negotiate. During the most important part, you're out of the loop. You wait. Your stomach constricts. Your fears expand. And of course, in my case, you continue to do your homework.

Finally, I was offered, and hastened to accept, seventy-five hundred dollars. Now, if only I could figure out what the hell this movie music stuff was all about.

A few days later, there's a knock on the door of our small apartment, and suddenly twenty reels of film and sound track are delivered. *The Swimmer* had finished shooting, it was filmed and edited, and now it was time for the composer to see it. I had to rent a Moviola, an instrument that lets you take a reel of 35-mm film and view it on a tiny screen. My first thought was "Where are we going to put all this? My mother doesn't even have room for a container of milk."

I'll never forget the day the Moviola was delivered. It's a big, bulky machine, and we lived on the second floor of a walkup. So here come these two huge men, each resembling Hulk Hogan, wrestling this giant machine up the stairs to our apartment. My principal aims at that moment were to write the best damn music since "Tara's Theme" and prevent these two men from getting double hernias.

I installed the instrument in our crowded living room. It would sleep nearby me, its unblinking eye keeping watch on my slumbers. If there was little space to spare in our living room before I moved in the Moviola, now there was *none*. We would have been ill advised to buy a canary. I put the Moviola at a right angle to my piano keyboard so I could sit on the bench, watch and compose, and swivel ninety degrees to study the film as it unreeled on the little screen.

I had to time each segment with a stopwatch. (That was easy, thanks to my sessions with Dr. Stopwatch.) I would then compose some music that fit the mood and action of the scene and the precise amount of time allotted. I'd time each scene, play something that sounded right, tape it, then try to adjust the length of the music, padding or trimming it to fit. In scoring a movie, as in life, timing is everything. When you're writing the music for a movie, 50 to 55 percent is in the quality of the music you create, your inspiration and talent. But there's a tremendous amount of work that is purely calculating minutes and seconds. You can write the greatest minute and thirty seconds, but if they only need a minute twenty-eight, you haven't done the job.

I couldn't help but think that if Frédéric Chopin had written the "Minute Waltz" and brought it to Sam Spiegel, he might hear big Sam berate him: "Freddy, I love it, it's catchy. But we only need fifty-eight seconds. Go home and try again."

They say that to succeed in life it is vital to be ambitious but fatal to appear so. To write movie music it's vital to keep your eye on the stopwatch, but it's fatal to appear so. You're trying to keep the music from *sounding* as if it's been written for time. You're trying to make it come to a graceful, inevitable end. You're trying to conceal the fact that they told you, "Remember, Marvin, one minute twenty-eight. No more."

That's the mechanical part of motion-picture scoring. The other is the more important part: the creative decisions on what kind of music you will write and where it will go. These decisions are usually made jointly by the composer and the director—and deciding where music should *not* go is just as important as deciding where it belongs. A composer can heighten some aspect of a scene, and music can also help its pacing. It can add more romance or more comedy. Music is an element that when properly used elevates a movie to heightened emotional levels. In John Williams's score for *Jaws*—with all those low basses—I still don't feel it's safe to go back into the water. There are alternatives as to what to highlight in any given scene. For example, in a chase scene the composer can simply accentuate the chase and provide accelerated music. Or he can mirror the fear of the characters who are on the run with "fear music." There might be notes held for a long time, the music very slow, allowing you to hear the panting of the fleeing characters. Or one can approach the scene from the perspective of the pursuer, determined to catch his prey. The composer has all these choices. Sure, it's a collaborative effort, and the director is extremely helpful in giving you his opinion and his ideas. But ultimately it's the composer who sets down the notes.

There I was, watching *The Swimmer* again and again, watching Burt Lancaster splashing, playing the piano against each scene until I found something I thought would be appropriate. The score was taking on a big, rather symphonic sound. So I wanted a massive tone. I wanted the audience to feel yearning and anguish, as each pool stop peels back part of the hero's life, revealing him as a fraud and a failure. I called on the size and power of a symphony orchestra to convey this man's pain.

Each afternoon after school, I returned to *The Swimmer* in our living room. I didn't write something wonderful every day. Some days, inspiration would elude me, and nothing worthwhile came out of my head. Maybe it was the chlorine. Well, so be it. Like Scarlett and Little Orphan Annie, I'd just wait for tomorrow.

I would get home at about four-thirty in the afternoon and immediately take care of all my homework, thus clearing the decks for *The Swimmer*. The composing was usually done in the evening, sometimes late into the night. Between the Moviola and the piano, I was making, if nothing else, a lot of noise. I loved working, and that love was being tested by a schedule that bordered on the maniacal. The deadline was grueling. The score had to be ready in no more than six weeks. Therefore, when I turned to my piano each night, I prayed that something special would come out of my head, flow through my fingers and onto the keyboard. I couldn't wait indefinitely for inspiration to strike. If necessary, I would have to rush inspiration along. If the Muse didn't come to Marvin, Marvin would have to pursue the Muse.

Writing music, like writing prose, is supposed to be lonely work. As somebody once said: "Writing is easy. You just stare at a blank sheet of paper till drops of blood form on your forehead." But it isn't all loneliness. There are occasional interruptions, some of them pretty dramatic. One night, while working late at my Moviola/piano setup, I was interrupted by a pounding on the door.

"Police, open up!"

"Police?"

I opened the door and found two officers wearing stern expressions.

"Do you know what time it is?" asked Cop No. 1.

"Well, yes—"

"Someone in the building complained that you're makin' too much noise," said Cop No. 2.

"They heard a lot of shouting," said Cop No. 1.

"That was Burt Lancaster," I said.

The officers looked around the room.

There was no Burt Lancaster.

"Listen, we have to warn you, if you don't stop the racket, we'll have to run you in for disturbing the peace."

Run me in? Arrest me? An artiste at work? A few innocent chords and you spend the night watching winos throw up on their sneakers?

"I'm writing my first movie score," I said proudly.

"Just knock it off," said Cop No. 2.

I sighed. This was God's way of saying, "Turn in, Marvin."

I continued on the score for weeks, working night and day, making real progress. My mother loved it, but she tended to love everything I wrote. President Kennedy used to say: "If I fell out of my chair, my father would say, 'Did you see how gracefully Jack fell on the floor?'" My mother gave me the same kind of uncritical approval. I mean, my hands could accidentally hit two notes on the piano and she would shout from the kitchen, "That sounds wonderful, Marvin. And do you want celery in your tuna fish salad?"

Despite the fact that the score to *The Swimmer* wasn't Hamlisch's Concerto in F, my father liked it, too. He saw in the serious, symphonic sound of my score that maybe my Juilliard years were paying off. He had once told me: "Marvin, no matter what you write in the end—be it pop, Broadway, films—what Juilliard is giving you will serve you well."

It is usual for the wise composer to phone his producer from time to time and play a few freshly minted pieces of music for him. Just to keep in touch. Just to let him know he is getting his money's worth. What did I know? I was a twenty-three-year-old kid. I didn't want him to hear bits and pieces in his office. I wanted to play the finished score in a projection room while he watched the film.

So a few weeks into my work, Sam Spiegel phones me. He is raging mad. Not just a little perturbed; I'm talking volcanic angry. All I could get from his side of the telephone conversation—and that's all there was—was that he was furious. I thought he was going to fire me on the spot, and for the life of me I couldn't figure out what I'd done wrong.

"Why haven't I heard anything yet? What the hell's going on?" he screamed.

Spiegel hadn't heard from me; ergo, he thought I hadn't been working on his movie. He didn't realize that I already had almost half the picture done. I promised to rush right over to his apartment and play what I'd written.

I hung up the phone, scooped the manuscript paper from the piano, scampered down the stairs, hailed a taxi, and headed for the St. Moritz. It wasn't until I got to his suite and played the music for the first four reels that Spiegel calmed down and turned into the charming man who raised his eyebrows instead of raising the roof.

He loved the music. He really did. And so the crisis passed. Or so I thought. A few days later, my physical system just about broke down, and my doctor ordered a battery of tests on my stomach. I was given an upper GI series which proved negative. But the terrible stomach pains continued intermittently, and some of them had me doubling over. I was told to take more liquid Maalox and try to get more rest. Well, I didn't know the meaning of the word rest. Panic, yes; rest, no. It just wasn't my style. Even when I was "taking it easy," most people thought I was on something. For me, quick was normal; fast forward was my mode of choice.

I finished the score, and luckily the pains subsided; it was time to fly to Hollywood. As I got ready to make the trip, the one thing I didn't really worry about was the music. I had other worries.

Before there was Erica Jong's *Fear of Flying*, there was mine. After all, if God had wanted us to fly, he wouldn't have given us economy class. Whenever I expressed any anxiety about soaring aloft, my father would prophesy that eventually, out of sheer necessity, I'd be taking planes all the time, without a moment's worry or hesitation. He proved to be right.

But then was then. So when Sam Spiegel dispatched me to Hollywood, I didn't hesitate for an instant. I booked myself on a train to Los Angeles.

California here I come. Slowly.

My mother saw me off at Grand Central with a veal cutlet sandwich. Just think, a train, a suitcase, and a veal cutlet sandwich. I'm talking about a world-class veal cutlet sandwich here, one with soggy, soggy white bread. That, my friends, is heaven. No dining car on the 20th Century Limited would dare to compete. It was the perfect start to a thrilling adventure on wheels. This would be the most exciting train ride since Jack Lemmon and Tony Curtis set off for Florida with an all-girl orchestra.

My train pulled out of Grand Central, heading first for Chicago before cutting across America to Flagstaff, Arizona, and then taking the home stretch to the City of Angels. My mother decided that since I was going to be gone from home, she would take the time to visit her brother, Ernst, and my Aunt Regina in Chicago. He met her plane there and was ready to drive her to their house.

"No," said my mother. "You must do me a favor, Ernst. First drive me to the train station." Never one to argue with his sister, he complied.

As my train pulled into Chicago's Union Station, there was my mother on the platform, holding aloft another veal cutlet sandwich for the next leg of my journey. But even though those veal cutlets kept my stomach happy, sixty hours and three thousand miles of clickety-clack, clickety-clack did something to a young guy impatient for his future to start. When I stepped off that train in California, I swore to myself that—despite my fear—my return trip would definitely be by air.

* * *

I couldn't wait to see Hollywood. Abe Burrows had said of it: "No matter how hot it gets in the daytime, there's nothing to do at night." Woody Allen once observed: "The only cultural advantage is you can make a right turn on a red light." Then there is Mel Brooks, who thinks the difference between Hollywood and yogurt is that yogurt has a living culture. Oscar Levant, another pianist who went west, remarked, "If you look under the tinsel, you find the *real* tinsel." Of course, Truman Capote liked to say, "It's a scientific fact that if you stay in California you lose one point off your IQ every year." As for Robert Redford, he said, "If you stay in Beverly Hills too long, you become a Mercedes." And Fred Allen's insult has become legendary: "It's a great place to live—if you're an orange."

I guess the best put-down of all is Neil Simon's. Extolling the wonderful weather, Neil said: "When it's a hundred in New York, it's seventy-two in Los Angeles. When it's thirty in New York, it's seventy-two in Los Angeles. However, there are six million interesting people in New York—and seventy-two in Los Angeles."

The other put-down that one heard, and continues to hear, is that the artistic triumphs happen in the East, the commercial ones happen in the West. People don't sit down to do quality work out there; they just try to make sure their work is salable. New York writers are artists; California writers play tennis. So goes the mythology.

Aside from matters of culture and literacy, I was nervous about Hollywood's reputation for its demeaning treatment of creative people. Gershwin had complained that they considered him hired help. I knew that Hollywood had driven Fitzgerald to drink and put Faulkner to work on a pharaoh epic. I knew that Jack Warner referred to his writers as "schmucks with Underwoods."

But despite my misgivings, I arrived in Hollywood with a sense of adventure. As God is my witness, I hurried to stand on the corner of Hollywood and Vine. For all I could see, I was standing on the corner of Walk and Don't Walk. Frankly, it looked like a mixture of Forty-second Street and a French penal colony.

I didn't actually like the California sun all that much. For one thing, I don't function well in a lot of heat. And as I stood on this fabled corner, it was *hot*. The next thing I discovered I disliked about Hollywood was that, unlike New York City, when you open the refrigerator for a Coke and find only an ice cube and a jar of mustard, you can't just run downstairs to the twenty-four-hour deli. You can't even find a cab to take you to the deli. In sunny Southern California, when you run out of Coke, you take the elevator to this subterranean garage, climb into your car, use a special remote to open the gate so you can get out of the underground maze, drive ten miles to an all-night Safeway, find a parking space, thread your way through the aisles, leave a trail of bread crumbs, grab a pack of Coke from the shelf, get on the express lane, and reverse the process.

A few days after I arrived in Hollywood, I went to Columbia Pictures on Gower and Sunset. I was told that my office was on the third floor. I soon confronted a door on which a wooden slat actually bore the words MARVIN HAMLISCH. I was quick to notice, however, that the slat slipped easily in and out of its brass holder. In and out. In and out. This sign of the ease of turnover in the Hollywood studio system was not lost on me.

I had hired two of Hollywood's best orchestrators to do the film. They were Jack Hayes and Leo Shuken. I had originally planned to conduct the score myself, though I had never done it before. A word of advice to artists in training: Learn all you can to prepare yourself for the challenges of life when they arrive. But when you find yourself facing the unknown, don't be afraid to shout, "HEL-LL-P!" They say the difference between genius and stupidity is that genius has its limits. The only thing worse than a stupid man is a stupid man who refuses to ask for help. So I asked and got Jack Hayes to conduct the score.

About a month after first coming to Los Angeles, we were about to record the music for the film. It was thrilling for me, because it was the first time I'd hear my music played by a full orchestra. Until then I had only heard the music in my head. The theme of *The Swimmer* was dramatic and despondent, but it was a theme that stayed with you. It was haunting. For three days, the giant orchestra played the score, and when all the music had been recorded, a number of the musicians came up to me and congratulated me on my work. Then it was over. The music was wedded to the film, and it was time for me to fly home to New York.

It was on that flight, as I recall, that I discovered the virtues of Valium. I returned without a tan, without a better backhand, and never having "done" lunch. Once back in New York, I waited impatiently for the film to be released. John Barrymore said, "You never know how short a month is until you pay alimony." Well, you never know how *long* a month is until you wait for your movie to open.

The Swimmer finally opened in the summer of 1968. As far as I was concerned, the title of the movie was *Music by Marvin Hamlisch*. I was thrilled when I saw my name up on the screen. There it was for everyone to see. Spelled perfectly. Sometimes I'd just go into the movie house and watch the first four minutes of the film, see my name, get a little giddy, throw away my popcorn, and retire from the theatre, having experienced my high for the day. Though the film itself did not do too well, my score got some marvelous reviews, particularly in the *Hollywood Reporter* and *Variety.*

The Swimmer brought me another job almost at once. I was about to take it when I was felled by another one of my terrific stomachaches. I quickly went to my doctor, who examined me and announced that I had a bleeding ulcer. "Do not pass Go. Go directly to hospital." I was twenty-four years old, with the feelings of immortality common to that age. I had never imagined I could get this sick this young. I was eager to prove myself with my first shot. It was all or nothing, a kind of roll of the dice to see if overnight I could become the next Max Steiner. This self-imposed pressure finally did me in.

As I lay in that hospital bed with a tube in my stomach, I had the time to think a few things through and figure out what the hell I was doing to myself. I was being whipsawed by my optimism and my pessimism. I was an optimist, like my mother: I expected the best and was crushed when events turned sour. Yet, like my father, I was a pessimist: I was terrified in situations where the outcome was in doubt.

I was anxious to "make it"—but I only made it to a semi-private room in a metropolitan hospital. And as you start to recover, you begin to make promises to yourself that you fully intend to carry out. After all, health is the basis of everything. "I will change my way of life. Oh, God, if You cure me, I will slow down, I won't gobble my food, I'll take better care of myself, I won't do as much. And I won't play rock songs during the silent devotion. Give me a break, God, and I'll make You proud of me."

I knew that when I got out of there, I would have to put all of these new realizations into some kind of perspective. Composing was meant to be a pleasure. But I couldn't continue like this. Without my perceiving it, my life had swung out of balance. It consisted of worry and work, anxiety and work, pushing and work, and work. I was preoccupied with my career and my future. I was always obsessed with looking ahead, planning every step, assessing every situation. I didn't consider that maybe the earth was round so that we couldn't see too far down the road.

On leaving the hospital, I found myself terribly depressed. I was sure the entire musical community thought of me as a "sickie." I could picture a billboard springing up on Sunset Boulevard: MARVIN HAMLISCH IS A HEALTH RISK. I had lost one movie to my ulcer. Where would my next job come from? Of course, I had promised I was going to change my ways, give up the life of double jeopardy—film and college—that had landed me in the hospital. Maybe I should just concentrate on school and get it over with. But the telephone rang. This time it was an offer to score a film for Woody Allen. I thought to myself: There's no way I'm going to get myself into this kind of mess again. I've got to finish school and live up to the promise I gave my father once and for all. I made my decision. A Woody Allen film? Me, Marvin Hamlisch?

Of course I said yes.

At that time, Woody Allen was not the much-praised director he is today. In fact, back then he was a brilliant monologist. I loved one line in which he said, "I really wanted to be an anarchist, but I didn't know where to go to register." I had been asked to write the score for the first film that he both wrote and directed: *Take the Money and Run*. Before our meeting, I went to a screening room to see the film. It was hilarious, and I loved the line when a girl says of her felonious boyfriend: "He never made the ten-most-wanted list. It's very unfair voting. It's who you know." So before I met Woody for the first time, I'm thinking: I'm going to be in stitches. He's going to be a million laughs, and I'll be rolling on the floor, biting at the chair leg. Well, not quite.

Woody was very quiet when I met him. He was quiet when I worked for him. He was quiet when I recorded the music for *Take the Money and Run* and then for *Bananas*. He hardly said a word to me unless he didn't like something I wrote. The only difficulty I had with our relationship was trying to tell when he was happy or unhappy, because he never really communicated with me.

Woody Allen is a genius, and he is one of America's foremost directors. The truth is, as he became the famous, much-admired filmmaker, he hardly ever used a composer for his films again. He relied instead on old recordings to score his movies. I sometimes wonder if working with me put that idea into his head.

The film community was slowly becoming aware of me, but the public itself had no idea who Marvin Hamlisch was. What I concluded at the time—and this may have been a giant mistake in the long run—was that if you wanted to make it as a Hollywood composer, the name of the game was "hits." What would put me on the map was writing a hit song for a picture. Everyone knew the name Henry Mancini. He wrote "Moon River" and "Days of Wine and Roses." Movies gave composers the chance to write songs that would live forever. And it gave them wonderful vehicles to bring them to the public. Do the words "White Christmas" ring a bell?

The record companies involved in the music of the movie industry were only interested in scores that had songs they could plug. I hadn't given a thought to any of this before, but now I was becoming caught in a web—although somewhere I knew better—of commercial considerations. I started thinking about writing film scores with "hit songs." It dominated my thoughts. I was transfixed. I dared myself to win at this Hollywood music game. I remembered the admonition of my mother: “Sometimes you’ve got to make elbows.”

The next movie I was offered was *Kotch*, a sort of geriatric comedy starring Walter Matthau and directed by his friend Jack Lemmon. He wanted a title song—finally, my chance for a hit. I didn’t think a title song called *Kotch* would work. Let’s face it, Sammy Cahn gets a picture with a great title like *Three Coins in the Fountain*. Sammy Fain gets *Love Is a Many Splendored Thing*. I get *Kotch*. Believe me, there’s not much you can rhyme with “Kotch,” and what you can rhyme with it is problematic.

Jack told me he was able to get Johnny Mercer to write the lyric, which was enough to bring me on board.

Let me tell you what it feels like to work with Johnny Mercer. All those years on *The Telephone Hour*, I had played dozens of famous songs with his name on them. He wrote the lyric for “Moon River” (which includes my favorite phrase: “my huckleberry friend”), “Blues in the Night,” “Dearly Beloved,” and “Something’s Gotta Give.”

He called and asked me to put the melody on audiotape and told me he’d get back to me soon. Five days later, he called again and said: “Okay, Marvin, I have it. It’s called ‘Life Is What You Make It.’ See what you think.” And what he had done, which no other lyricist I ever worked with before had ever done, was to come up with five—count ’em, five—different sets of lyrics; five complete versions of the song, each perfectly married to the melody. Then he said, “Marvin, take whichever you like. Feel free to take a little bit of version one, a little of version two . . .”

No vanity, take what you like. I cannot tell you how disarming it is to be confronted with such a total absence of ego in the music field. I was dumbfounded. But that’s Johnny Mercer for you.

* * *

Well, what happened is that *Kotch* came out, and it wasn't a huge success at the box office, though it did respectable business. The song, Johnny Mercer notwithstanding, was considered middle of the road, which is the kiss of death for radio stations. This was not the way to make it onto the charts. I had a good song but no cigar. Back to the drawing board. I had half-forgotten about *Kotch*, which by now had petered out of existence. It had become a sort of distant memory. I already had three new songs in the works.

Then, on a February morning in 1972, I received a special-delivery letter. I was astonished. I was shocked. No, I wasn't drafted. It was a letter notifying me that I had been nominated for a Golden Globe Award for *Kotch*. I could hardly believe it. I didn't even know what a Golden Globe was. I discovered that the Golden Globe is an award given by the Hollywood Foreign Press Association. The phone didn't stop ringing. Friends were ecstatic for me. I suddenly realized that this was major news. Of course, it never occurred to me that we had a chance to win. It was predestined that we would lose to the theme from *Shaft*, the big hit that year.

Reread those last couple of sentences. Typical Hamlisch. Here I am, up for a Golden Globe Award—my first serious nomination ever—and I've already thrown in the towel, convinced there's no way I can win. Why couldn't I just smell the coffee without complaining about the caffeine? Would I ever learn to accept the rewards of my work for what they were, no more, no less?

The evening arrived for the Golden Globes, and because Johnny Mercer was ill, I escorted his wife. Otherwise, I would have gone alone, since I wasn't seeing anyone special during those days except my gastroenterologist. With Mrs. Mercer on my arm and some chewable Maalox tablets in my pocket, I readied myself to endure the ceremonies.

We're at our own table for *Kotch*—Walter Matthau and Jack Lemmon and the rest. Our movie had received quite a few nominations. But to everyone's dismay, we're losing in one category after another. Jack Lemmon was growing increasingly upset. It was a kind of mock agitation. There was only one award left. The one for Best Song.

Jack Lemmon swiveled around in his chair and eyed me:

"Marvin, if you don't win, I'm going to kill you."

"What? Why?"

"Because we've got to have a party, and in order to have a party, you've got to actually *win* something."

"Not a prayer," I said. "The song is 'Shaft.' Forget it, Jack. It's over."

I tell him this, assuring him that we haven't a ghost of a chance, when the presenter reels off the list of nominated songs. Then it was time for the envelope. Jack's eyes were blazing by now. He's all over me, whispering admonitions in my left ear.

"No way, Jack!"

And then I hear a voice in my right ear:

"The winner is 'Life Is What You Make It' by Johnny Mercer and Marvin Hamlisch."

I rose from my chair as the lights lit up my startled face. I was being smothered by Jack's kisses, and I stumbled toward the dais.

I had no speech prepared. I was so stunned I doubted I could talk, anyway. I knew all they allowed was about thirty seconds, but there I was, totally unable to control my excitement and my thoughts. I am thanking *everyone*. I thanked Walter Matthau, Jack Lemmon, Johnny Mercer, the producer, the director, my mother, my father, my piano teacher, the musicians, the prop men, and, of course, my rabbi.

I'm saying, "You know, I'm just a kid from New York, and I never dreamed I'd get the chance to work with Johnny Mercer . . ." And I'm fighting back tears. "And I'm glad my parents could be here . . ." I continue burbling along as the floor manager is desperately signaling me to get off. They tell me it was probably the longest speech in the history of the Golden Globes.

Can lightning strike twice? I can't believe it, but a couple of weeks later we're nominated for an Academy Award. I knew exactly what *that* was. I didn't need anyone to tell me how ecstatic I should be.

For this, I bought a new tuxedo, flew my parents out from New York, rented a limo, and we royally made our way to the night of nights. I even went so far as to give up the idea—me, Marvin Hamlisch—of the foregone conclusion of defeat and let myself enjoy the reverie of imagining what it would be like to win. Even with the odds against me, I sat there feeling expectant and impossibly hopeful that it actually might happen. I later learned that this kind of wishful thinking is common to all nominees.

It seemed like days before they got to the Best Song category. The presenter endlessly ambled through the five nominated songs. I was on the edge of my chair, ready to run up the aisle. Get ready, cameras, here I come.

But the certainty died as I heard the words: "And the winner is 'Shaft.'"

I could tell the camera was still focused on me, and I had to wear a look of good fellowship no matter what. Some of the best acting takes place right after the announcement of the Best Actor awards. And the Best Song awards, too. I had come close to winning it all. But because I hadn't, I slid back. The only thing I could think about was that I was a loser. I should have been telling myself: Just keep going, don't look behind you, don't look left, don't look right, just keep moving. Excelsior.

If experience is the name we give to our mistakes, I've certainly gained a lot of experience. Because it has taken me a lifetime to realize that it's in the *doing* that we receive the satisfaction of knowing we've done our best, not in the adulation. Wasn't this really what my father had wanted me to learn—that my music didn't need to win an award, but rather, to be true to itself and worthy? That was the goal to strive for. Even if *The Swimmer* score wasn't revolutionary, it was musically substantial. When I listen to it now, I can still honestly say that I never compromised. I think I owe that kind of musical integrity to those fifty minutes on the roof and my teachers at Juilliard.

Her name was Frances S. Goldstein. She was an irascible old woman who always had a cigarette in her mouth. She was tough, but she taught me more about music theory than anyone before or since. And when I had finished my scores for *The Swimmer* and *Kotch*, I thought it would be wonderful to share them with her. I wondered if she ever went to a movie. Her class at Juilliard was her life, that narrow room in which she kept emphasizing what was good and what was bad harmonically. If she gave you a check on one of your papers, you knew she meant it. If Miss Goldstein said you had done well, it wasn't said lightly to reassure you. You had done well.

I dearly wanted her approval now. I wanted her to know that I hadn't forsaken or betrayed my musical training. I needed that gold star at the top of my homework assignment. With all that was happening to me, I needed her to reassure me I was on the right track. I was hungry for the approval of the heretofore aloof Miss Goldstein and wanted her to see that I was capable of doing serious work.

I telephoned her and said: "Miss Goldstein, I'd love to have you listen to the music I wrote. I really think it's good."

"Marvin, I don't have time to listen to this music of yours. I'm very, very busy."

"But don't you even have time for a cup of coffee?" I asked. "I could bring the music with me."

"No, no, no, no," she insisted.

I was terribly disappointed. I wanted her to know that I understood her values, her virtues, her commitment. She may have been out of touch with the outside world, but in that world she created in her classroom, she believed wholly in what she did. And I was envious of that. I needed to have that in *my* life. That narrow classroom was an honest place where she devoted herself to the highest standards of music. I needed to get back into that room.

Years later, I learned that Miss Goldstein was in the hospital with cancer. A tiny woman who had always weighed about ninety pounds, she was not expected to live. As I looked down at her frail body in the hospital bed, it was hard to recall the teacher who seemed so tough and formidable at Juilliard.

She told me that her students didn't visit her, and this did not surprise me. She was a killer in the classroom and not immensely likable. Now she could barely speak. Those ever-present cigarettes had ravaged her throat and finally done her in.

We talked of the old days at Juilliard and of my new career. Finally, it was time to go.

"Good-bye, Miss Goldstein," I said, and started for the door.

"Marvin—" she said.

"Yes, Miss Goldstein?"

"I really should have taken time for that cup of coffee."

6.

ANN-MARGRET, GROUCHO, AND ME

At last I graduated from Queens College. It may have taken more years than I care to think, but at least I had lived up to my promise to my father. And it felt good to have a degree, to have read some first-rate books, and get a chance to sit in a classroom, the library, and not always on a piano bench. But I must confess that it slowly started to rankle that I had come so close to the Oscar with *Kotch* and hadn't won.

You know by now that I am an inveterate New Yorker, but it began to dawn on me, that to write music for films, it might be better to be where the film studios are. That was it! I had to return to Hollywood. (Notice I didn't say *move* there.) I figured that a couple of parties, with some big film producers and directors, might land me the kind of films that were sure-fire winners.

Well, Rome wasn't built in a day, and I discovered that neither was my career in Hollywood. Although I started to get known and make friends in the film industry, the films I actually worked on at first weren't exactly my idea of blockbusters.

In fact, they weren't anybody's idea of blockbusters. I was restless and wondering why I had come out here in the first place.

Then, suddenly, two people came into my life who would become very close friends of mine: one of them was Ann-Margret, who wanted me to create a new nightclub act for her, and the other was none other than the inimitable Groucho Marx. And although this wasn't what I had uprooted myself from New York for, there *are* some offers you can't refuse.

I had first met Ann-Margret in 1970, when Allan Carr, who early in his career was her manager, introduced us. He liked my music. Now he wanted to know if I would be willing to create a new act for Ann-Margret. I had seen her perform in Las Vegas, and she certainly was a knockout, ravishingly beautiful, high-powered, and energetic. But that's not why I wanted to work with her. I think I sensed, like the rest of the American public, that there was more to Ann-Margret than that. Underneath all that extravaganza, there was a special quality to her.

Not only did she always give 100 percent, but you could tell that she really cared about the people she was working with, and more important, she gave every bit of herself to her audience, and meant it.

Every time I saw her, in a movie or on a television interview, it was her genuineness that captured me. There just didn't seem to be one mean bone in her incredible body. Matter of fact, I don't think I've ever heard one nasty story about her, a record matched only by Mother Teresa and Emily Dickinson.

My instincts were correct. She had enormous Swedish resilience: she loved to rehearse until she got it right, over and over, no matter how long it took, and she adored being with and talking to the dancers she worked with. She never played the "star," never once came late—she was just "one of the guys." She could be funny at times, and as I got to know her better, I started to come up with all kinds of new ideas that would reveal *this* Ann-Margret to her nightclub audiences.

They say that Las Vegas has fifty stars and one sauce. But people don't go there for the food, anyway. They go there to gamble and to see the shows. Ann-Margret wowed them, all right, but I knew there was something missing. There was too much glitter and glamour. But Walter Painter, her choreographer, and I knew we could do more than that—we could make everyone in the room fall in love with her.

Las Vegas nightclub acts tend to follow a certain formula. Yes, the opening number has to give them what they want: Ann-Margret in hot pants, doing a torrid disco number astride a motorcycle. Then comes in short order: the obligatory mid-tempo number, the change of costumes, the chance for everyone to say to each other: "She looks fantastic." There wasn't enough of the unexpected. It was time to play against the usual image she conveyed. It was time, once and for all, to "humanize" Ann-Margret.

The third number had to be pivotal. Yes, it was in the third number where Walter and I decided we had to make our move. It was a simple thing. Others had been famous for it—it was the fundamental issue of human contact. So I said to myself: Let's take this ravishingly beautiful star who seems so remote and removed from mere mortals and bring her down to earth.

"What if we have her come down into the audience?"

That would be like Venus stepping off her pedestal to cavort with the earthlings.

But there was a problem: Ann-Margret insisted then on being totally scripted. It was a habit that came from working in movies. For all the impact of her act, it lacked spontaneity. Walter and I were about to change all that. We chose the song "Take a Little One-Step" from *No, No, Nanette*, the Vincent Youmans musical of the twenties. It was a *Hello, Dolly!*—type number.

What was needed was for her to actually come down into the audience, talk to people, and find a man to dance with. I arranged the number—it ran a full eight minutes—and brought it to Ann-Margret. You would have thought I had brought a bacon-and-tomato sandwich to my rabbi. On Yom Kippur.

"No no no no no," she said emphatically.

It's not often I get a five-no answer. But I knew that this was right for her. I now fought hard for what was best for Ann-Margret.

"All you have to do is go up to a guy in the audience," I said, "ask him where he's from, and then ask him if he'd like to dance. It's no big deal."

"Marvin," she said, "I'm nervous about ad-libbing."

"All you have to do is talk to two or three guys. From then on it's a piece of cake."

When we first rehearsed this number, she was wary of it. But she did have faith in Walter and me. Slowly, she got more comfortable.

Well, opening night arrived, and she got nervous about it all over again. Yet the moment she made her way to the first balding businessman from Omaha, she was a natural.

The woman who was so nervous about being spontaneous turned into a master of the ad lib. The Ann-Margret who had to be completely scripted became a mistress of extempore. She became very adept at chatting. She bubbled, and the audience could tell that she was really enjoying herself—that she liked them.

She talked to the audience—and talked and talked and talked. They were not used to this from her—and they loved it.

The song grew longer and longer. We had created a monster. My hunch was right. The friendliness and true warmth of this wonderful woman had finally revealed itself.

And with that act, our cherished friendship began. We have developed a trust between us that is one of the things I value most. Hard to believe, but for all her success, her fame, her image, Ann-Margret is one of the most down to earth people I have ever met. We have been through a lot together. Lots of good times, like those wonderful Christmas parties she and her husband, Roger Smith, would give, surrounded by family and friends. Their home is warm, cozy, and loving, and I don't think I've seen too many more beautiful Christmas trees. Me personally, I seemed always to concentrate on her mother's Swedish meat-balls.

There were a lot of tough times, too. I can't help remembering that when my mother lay dying in a New York hospital, Ann-Margret flew in from Las Vegas, where she had performed that evening. She came to my mother's bedside and to comfort me. She returned that same night to do another show.

Nor can I forget the horror I felt when I heard the news of her terrible accident while performing at the Sahara Tahoe in 1972: She had dropped from a moving scaffold during her opening number. I rushed to UCLA hospital to find her battered, her jaw wired shut, multiple bruises covering her face. Roger had taped black paper over the mirrors in the room so she couldn't see what she looked like. Ann-Margret was a fighter. She was determined to recover. Unbelievably, her first concern was for her dancers; they were now out of work, and she was worried about them. At night, when Roger left the room to go home for a few hours' sleep, I would come to the hospital with a coffee malted and a straw for her, and we would just sit there, in the quiet of the hospital, not having to say a word. There would be many operations to restore those glorious cheekbones. It would take many months for her to heal. I wondered, like everyone else, if she would ever quite look the same. But as she lay in that bed—no Bob Mackie gown, no jewelry, no theatrical hairdo, no makeup—I saw in front of me simply the most beautiful woman I had ever known.

Since then there's been lots of laughing between us. She calls me "Hamlisch." I call her "Slugger."

I have a favorite recollection from the first night when Walter and I saw the act we had created for her at the Hilton Hotel in Las Vegas—a hotel, by the way, that has the best coffee malteds in the West. Ann-Margret's dressing room seemed like the biggest apartment I'd ever seen: a giant living room, a luxurious bedroom, a mammoth bath with mirrored ceilings, yet. Just like West Eighty-first Street.

Then the word came over the intercom: "Ann-Margret, onstage, please."

"Marvin," she said, "come with me." She took my arm.

We headed for the private elevator beside her dressing-room door. We rode down in silence. There was all the allure: the $30,000 gown, the fascination of the place. I knew that elevator door would open to more fantasy, for this was what Vegas was about.

The elevator descended, came to a stop, and the doors slid open. At first, I thought that the elevator had stopped at the wrong floor. I couldn't believe my eyes—the steaming, hot, noisy, smelly, garbage-laden kitchen. So much for my fantasy of glittery entrances onto nightclub stages.

Trying to preserve my poise, here I was walking arm in arm with America's great movie star, across a linoleum floor, dodging flying eggshells, soiled lettuce leaves, and those damned tiny umbrellas that are a must in your mai tais. The room smelled of garlic. Waiters shouted their orders in five languages, and cooks barked at their helpers.

"More mashed potatoes."

"Get the soup."

"Cancel the salmon."

"Hey, Pedro, I'm quitting. I just got my green card!"

And I reflected that nobody would believe that Ann-Margret, in order to get to the footlights, was actually making her way through this combat zone. It was a jolting experience and in many ways a maturing one. I suddenly took it in: For every delectable moment in life, there would always be the harsh smell of reality. The greater the achievement, the more slippery the linoleum floor. Yes, there are a lot of routes to success in life, but many of them lead through the kitchen.

I also had the rare good fortune to work for a man whom the world considers a legend and whom I did not meet until the twilight years of his life. And though he loved to sing, trust me, he never won an award for his vocal abilities.

Fade up on my rented apartment in Los Angeles. It is a smoggy autumn day (sound of hacking cough). It is 1972, and I am dividing my time between the *New York Times* and Mallomars. There is a knock at the door, I open it and find a lady who introduces herself:

"I'm Erin Fleming. I'm your neighbor," she says. "I've heard you playing the piano. I'm Groucho Marx's secretary." She was also his confidante and companion.

Groucho had long been an idol of mine. In fact, it was David Steinberg who once said: "The most influential people who ever lived were Alexander the Great, Jesus Christ, and Groucho Marx. And not necessarily in that order."

Miss Fleming unexpectedly confided in me:

"There's something I want to tell you. Groucho is growing increasingly frail and senile. He's in his eighties now. He's out-lived Chico and Harpo and most of his friends and show-business pals. I think it would be very helpful to have him get out in the world. I'd like to get someone to let him sing around the piano with his friends. So I thought of you."

I agreed that might prove excellent therapy. Inconceivable. I was going to be working and playing with Groucho Marx.

So I reported to his house in Beverly Hills and found that this most famous cynic and curmudgeon was really very gentle. He could still be the witty crank that lit a thousand anecdotes. Like the time when a priest approached him and said: "I want to thank you for all the joy you've brought into the world," and Groucho replied, "I want to thank you for all the joy you've taken out of it."

You have to understand something. I never knew my grand-parents, from either side. They all died in Vienna in the war, victims of the Nazis. Groucho was this sweet, funny, elderly, Jewish man; he was like the grandfather I never had.

First he dove into his shelves and drawers and produced the sheet music (held precariously together by tape) for some of the songs he sang in his movies, shows, and vaudeville acts. I'd start playing these oldies, and Groucho began singing them. It was incredible that when it came to the lyrics of his beloved songs, the elderly Groucho still remembered just about all of them. When he recounted vintage anecdotes, sometimes he'd have trouble recalling bits of information, or he'd tell me the same joke three times in one day. But with song lyrics, his memory never failed. I could see that singing the songs he loved was really renewed pleasure for Groucho. His face would light up, and so would his cigar. Soon I was asked to play at one of his parties, knowing all too well that Groucho needed me there when the time came for him to get up and sing a few songs. I was, by now, the resident Groucho accompanist.

Groucho knew everybody in Hollywood. So when he gave a party, the guest list was, to say the least, impressive. All these heavyweight stars were like kids, grinning ear to ear, when Groucho leaned against the piano and sang "Hello, I Must Be Going" or "Timbuctoo" or "Lydia, the Tattooed Lady." And then there were the times when he wasn't singing but sat alone with me, telling those marvelous stories.

"As a composer, you'll appreciate this, Marvin. Irving Berlin once wrote a song called 'Stay Down Here Where You Belong.' It was a terrible song. Awful. But I always liked it and used to sing it a lot. And one day Irving calls me up and says, 'Groucho, I'll pay you whatever you want *not* to sing "Stay Down Here Where You Belong."'"

I never tired of these gems. I sometimes risked bothering him: "Groucho, tell me some more. Know anything about Gershwin?"

"Gershwin?" Groucho asked. "I got plenty to tell you about Gershwin. I knew George like the back of my hand. Gershwin was invited to every 'A' party in Hollywood. He always played the piano. And I wanted him to come to a party I was giving. And I *definitely* wanted him to play the piano. But I didn't want it to look like I was depending on him. Or using him. So I invited everybody in town to the party, including his brother, Ira." Groucho and Ira were great pals.

"But I didn't invite George," Groucho continued. "So the night before the party, George calls me up and says, 'Groucho, I don't understand this. You lost my address or something?' And I say, 'No, George, I'm sick of it. People always invite you to their parties because they want you to play the piano. They exploit you. I don't want to do that. Don't come. These people will take advantage of you. They'll have you playing all evening long. Please, George, don't show up.'"

"So what happened, Groucho?" I asked.

"What happened?" he answered. "The next evening, George Gershwin crashed my party and played the piano for six hours. You gotta hand it to George, he wasn't bad."

Groucho was a master of these stories, and furthermore, he responded magnificently to our new regime of singing, parties, and more singing. He was enjoying every minute of it. He loved the limelight and was invigorated by it. And a new idea arose: "Why doesn't Groucho do some concerts? He could go out and tell the same stories he's been telling to his dinner guests."

In order to do this, we needed to make sure that the eighty-two-year-old Groucho would get enough help so that his memory would not fail him. Certain key words were written on three-by-five-inch index cards that would serve to cue him into his anecdotes, and he would have me at the piano so he could sing his songs. If he strayed in telling the stories, as he might from time to time, I would be able to get him back on track, since by now I knew them all by heart.

Our first concert was at Iowa State University. A student met us at the airport and drove us to the campus. And when we got out of the car, the reaction was explosive. I had never seen anything to compare with the way those kids flocked to him. Like he was an endangered species. Which he was. Talk about a megastar. These kids worshiped him from the days of the Marx Brothers movies; they remembered the greasepaint mustache, the crouched walk, the leering eyes. Or they may have seen reruns of his TV quiz show *You Bet Your Life*. (One guest on the show was a woman who had given birth to twenty-two children. "I love my husband," she explained defensively. "I love my cigar, too," said Groucho, "but I take it out once in a while.")

There was a tradition at Iowa State that every time the chapel bells tolled the hour, a girl could kiss whatever guy was handy.

Groucho had the time of his life. Every time the hour tolled, he was kissed by more women than a sultan in heat. Ask not for whom the bell tolls. They tolled for Groucho. Kisses rained down on him. Me? Unnoticed, I was standing there with my hands in my pockets, saying: "Excuse me. Anybody here for a pianist?" As for the concert itself in Iowa, it was simply hysterical.

The most tumultuous concert was at Carnegie Hall on October 31, 1972. What a love fest that was. The evening began with my coming onstage to play an overture. To my amazement, when I looked down into the audience, I was startled to see no less than a hundred and fifty Grouchos out there—dozens of them sporting the infamous Groucho masks.

The opening remarks were made by Dick Cavett. He recalled his first meeting with Groucho. "Groucho asked me to walk down Fifth Avenue with him," Dick recalled, "and we stopped every so often so he could insult a doorman." Groucho unexpectedly invited Dick to lunch with him. Dick related the famous story of Groucho's aborted attempt to use the swimming pool at an anti-Semitic country club. Groucho asked, "Since my daughter's only half Jewish, can she go in up to her knees?"

Then Dick introduced Groucho to the audience, along with his movie identities: Rufus T. Firefly, Dr. Hugo Z. Hackenbush, Otis B. Driftwood, and Capt. Geoffrey T. Spaulding. Groucho received a standing ovation that lasted over four minutes. I played several choruses of "Hooray for Captain Spaulding" as the applause kept building.

Groucho entered holding a violin. He explained that he knew that Jack Benny had played Carnegie Hall. He then threw the violin down on the ground and stomped on it.

And that, my friends, was only the beginning.

He talked of his career in show business, and with his

wonderful flair for hyperbole, the reminiscences were hilarious and bittersweet.

He told of how he had gotten his first break. “I saw an ad in the *Morning World*. It read: ‘Boy wanted to sing.’ I ran all the way from Ninety-third Street to Thirty-third Street, ran up five flights of stairs, and knocked on the door. And a man came to the door wearing a woman’s outfit. Not entirely, just lipstick. And I realized that this was the profession for me.”

Then Groucho went on about his family.

“I had an uncle named Julius,” said Groucho, explaining the source of his real first name. “He was well over four feet tall.” He told of his adopted sister, Polly. “She wasn’t a bad-looking girl, but her rear end stuck way out. You could play pinochle on it.” He related how another uncle would come to their house and cut their toenails for twenty-five cents. “Finding this inadequate to make a living,” said Groucho, “since it was winter and very cold, he got a job setting fire to hotels in the Catskills.”

Groucho was very touchy about the critics. He remembered a particularly wounding reviewer in Chicago when he and his brothers were playing there. The critic was Percy Hammond of the *Chicago Tribune*, and Groucho remembered his derisive review of their act. It had said: “The Marx Brothers and their various relatives ran around the stage for almost an hour yesterday afternoon. Why I’ll never understand.”

“During the Second World War,” said Groucho, “the *Chicago Tribune*’s foreign correspondent had died. And they had to get a new guy. And somebody suggested sending Percy Hammond over. And Ring Lardner said, ‘No, no, you can’t do that. Suppose he didn’t *like* the war.’”

Groucho recalled *Monkey Business*, a movie he had made at Paramount. He related that when Rudolf Hess flew to England on his impromptu peace mission and reported to Churchill, the prime minister was screening *Monkey Business*. Groucho recounted how Churchill told his aide: "Tell Hess to come back when the movie's over." He remembered a great line from the film that the censors had removed, as they did many of Groucho's best. Groucho tells Thelma Todd: "I know, you're a misunderstood woman who's been getting nothing but dirty breaks. Well, we can clean and tighten your brakes, polish your frame, and oil your joints, but you'll have to stay in the garage overnight."

The audience loved him, worshiped him, and he truly enjoyed being back on a stage. He also seemed to be having the most fun when he sang. Occasionally, he would turn to me in mock agitation after an arpeggio annoyed him and say: "I don't think that was necessary."

"Shall we take another crack at it?" I kidded him. And we would begin the song again.

Groucho was incapable of holding a serious conversation; he could not be solemn if it killed him. He seemed to have a compulsion to mock everything and everybody, which may be why his sessions around the piano—in his living room or on the concert stage—proved such good therapy. This was just what he needed to regain some of the lilt of his early years.

And yes, Groucho was a passionate man. Like other famous curmudgeons, from Dorothy Parker to Oscar Levant, he would sacrifice anyone for a laugh. But there was a great humanness to the man. Whenever I think of him, I recall an exchange in *A Night at the Opera*. Groucho and the inevitable Margaret Dumont are ascending the gangplank of a luxury liner.

"Are you sure you have everything, Otis?" she says.

"I haven't had any complaints yet," says Groucho.

I never had any complaints about you, either.

I miss you, Groucho. We all do.

* * *

What I also started to miss was getting back to writing my own music. I was twenty-eight years old, still in California, and waiting for what I had come out there to happen. But just as I was thinking of packing it in and going back to New York, Ray Stark, whom I'd worked for on *Funny Girl*, unexpectedly telephoned me. He wanted to see me. My instincts told me that this was finally going to lead somewhere.

And I was right.

7.

THE WAY WE WERE/THE STING

Ray Stark told me he was going to give me my "big break." He wanted me to work with the legendary John Huston on his upcoming movie *Fat City*. I had long admired Huston's brilliant work: *The Maltese Falcon*, *The Treasure of the Sierra Madre*, *The African Queen*. If there was ever someone I was sure I could learn from, it was John Huston. I counted the days prior to meeting the master, but I never did. I never met *anybody*: no one outside of the accounting department.

Not only did I not meet John Huston, but the music for *Fat City* was almost entirely what they call "source music," music that's coming from a radio or a jukebox or some other source in the scene. So the young composer had little to do but go down to Nashville and record some country and western groups doing their own songs. This was not exactly stretching my musical horizons. In fact, the hardest part of this whole job was making sure that the W-2 forms I took down there would be signed by the musicians. I had suddenly gone from being a composer to being an accountant, and that's the part I worried about most. Accounting is a noble calling, but it's not me. It's always been a good arrangement: Price Waterhouse doesn't write music, and I don't conduct audits.

The easy part of my assignment was recording the country and western music, most of which was authentic and written by other writers. I also tossed off a few minor songs for the film. When I returned to Hollywood, W-2s in hand, I couldn't wait for Ray Stark to hear what I had done.

"Okay, I'm finished," I announced. "I have everything recorded. And it came in under budget." It was that last line that perked up all ears. No one had bothered to *listen* to the tape or to tell me if they liked the music or not. All they knew was I brought it in on time and under budget. And I had the W-2s to prove it.

Eventually, Ray Stark must have listened to the tapes, because later he told me that he liked a couple of the original songs I had written. And then I don't think I talked to him for six or seven months, until one day he called me:

"Marvin, I'm working on a new picture which needs a theme song. I think this is up your alley, and I'd like to give you a chance. But you haven't got the track record yet, Marvin, and the director wants you to do this on spec." Which meant that if he didn't care for the song, it was no harm, no foul. I'd be here today, gone tomorrow. If, on the other hand, he liked it, I would get the job of scoring the whole movie.

What Stark didn't tell me till the end of the conversation was that the director was Sydney Pollack, the stars were Barbra Streisand and Robert Redford, and the movie was *The Way We Were*. For this I would certainly work "on spec," and I must confess that I sensed from the beginning that this was going to be my watershed in the movies. The intimidation of writing for Barbra Streisand was matched by the remarkable challenge. I feed off opportunities like this; the higher the stakes, the greater the stimulation.

I couldn't wait to get to the piano, and I put in weeks and weeks of struggle to find the right theme. How many *The Way We Were*'s there were, I cannot tell you. Unlike Juilliard, where a jury of three decided whether I would maintain my scholarship, here there was a jury of one. Never was there a more harsh critic of my work than me.

The film *The Way We Were* was a love story about a serious Jewish girl, a student radical, who falls for the most gorgeous WASP on campus. He spends his time writing and is not interested in politics. Opposites attract. They meet, fall madly in love, start a family, but then, finally, predictably, go their own way.

I wanted to reflect all this: the sorrow and despondency and pain of the relationship and its outcome, the frustration and yearning of the woman in the relationship, and the star-crossed nature of it all. Now, you may recall from some distant music-appreciation course that the major mode is the "happy one" and the minor mode is the "sad one." Although this song would reflect a heartbreaking story, I decided to write it in the major mode. By doing this, I tried to give a sense of hope to this tragic story.

And no matter what I was doing, from picking up my laundry to eating breakfast at a nearby I-HOP to pushing my cart down the aisles at Safeway, I could hear Barbra's voice in my head and recall how wonderful she sounds when she holds certain notes. I wanted to give her the notes that let her soar. I was determined not to write something drippingly sentimental. To be honest, my first attempts were in that direction. I'd work for three hours, then leave the piano, and try again the next day. At night, my dreams were accompanied by a soundtrack, and it was always Streisand's voice doing the singing.

Next morning, I'd give it another go.

You may wonder how I knew when I'd written the "right"

melody. I can only say that one day I wrote a melody that just *got to me*. I can't give you a musical explanation of why one melody is better than another—I either respond or I don't. The years of theory and harmony at Juilliard can take you just so far. One's response is not rational or technical. It goes beyond that. When I feel the emotional tug, when I react the way I hope the audience will, then I know I've got it.

It reminds me of the apocryphal story about Michelangelo. Someone asked the great artist: "How do you sculpt an elephant?" and he replied: "I get this slab of marble and I chip away everything that doesn't look like an elephant to me. What's left is an elephant." In the same way, seated at my piano, I chip away everything that doesn't feel like the correct melody. What's left, hopefully, is the right one.

I thought the song had everything. Well, not quite. Now it needed a lyric. Ray Stark got Alan and Marilyn Bergman, who were on the top rung of movie lyricists and had a long-standing relationship with Streisand. These were the writers who in 1968 had won an Oscar and a Golden Globe for "The Windmills of Your Mind." They were nominated again the following year for "What Are You Doing the Rest of Your Life?" and received Oscar nominations in the five successive years.

The lyrics couldn't have been better. The song completed, not your best three singers that ever lived went to sell their song to the best singer of them all. If I said I wasn't nervous during this critical audition, I would be nothing less than a liar.

I arrived at the Streisand house. It was a big, cavernous place, a feast for the eyes. I sat at the piano and waited. After what seemed like forever, she came downstairs. We reminisced about *Funny Girl*, those sleepless nights in Boston, and those chocolate-glazed doughnuts from Horn & Hardart. The Hemingway moment arrived. I started to play the introduction and then went into the song. And it was then that Barbra Streisand first heard "The Way We Were."

She loved it, but she made a very important suggestion. The third line of the melody I had written brought the notes down the scale, but Barbra's infallible instincts made her want the melody to take off and rise. We tried it, and she was right. It was one of those rare, exciting moments when a collaboration works perfectly.

It came as somewhat of a shock to me, therefore, when on the way home, Alan suggested in the car that "maybe we could do even better." There were still several months before the film editing was finished, so he thought there was time to go back to the drawing board.

I couldn't believe this was happening to me. I had poured my heart into what I had written, and I just didn't think that I had a better "The Way We Were" in me. There was absolutely no way to rethink the whole song. I am told that the executives at one top ad agency make it a practice when a client turns down a proposal for an ad campaign to declare: "All right, we'll give you our second-best idea."

So the Bergmans and I wrote a second "The Way We Were," more complex in structure, with a more complicated melody. Barbra liked "The Way We Were, II." It had the virtue of being fresh to her ear.

Sydney Pollack then did a very savvy thing. He put *both* songs on the sound track so that you could hear each of them with the same scene. This gave everyone a clear sense of how each of the songs would register. The original version seemed to work best, and Barbra agreed. (Interestingly enough, after all these years, Barbra has released "The Way We Were, II" on her CD entitled *For the Record*. Now you can decide for yourself.)

With this behind me, I finished the score for the film. Barbra and I met to discuss exactly what the song would sound like when it was orchestrated. After the meeting, I did some checking with other conductors about recording sessions they had done with Barbra. I was told that sometimes, during recording sessions, she would ask for changes. I wanted no glitches. Not wanting to take any chances, I decided to prepare three different orchestrations: One would be written very romantically to surround the vocal; one would be written with less romance and more introspection; and the third would be a combination of these approaches. I called these versions A, B, and C.

On the day of the recording session, I walked over to her and found her, like me, ready and anxious to attack the task at hand. We were two professionals settling down to work—and I liked my newfound status. To think that only a few years ago I was a rehearsal pianist, playing "People" for her. Now, at the age of twenty-nine, I had an orchestra in front of me and Barbra Streisand behind me in a soundproof booth. She was going to sing *my* song.

I had dreamed about this. I had heard her voice in my sleep dozens of times, hitting the notes I had written, taking them further than I could ever have imagined. But when the introduction started at the session and I suddenly heard that incredible voice in my earphones, I realized she had even surpassed, right there in front of me, what I had heard her do inside me. I doubt any other singer could have done that.

But suddenly her voice faded. "Marvin, I'm having trouble here with the orchestration. Let's take a thirty-minute break."

"There's no need for a break. Just give me ten seconds, Barbra." I turned to the orchestra and said: "Plan B, boys."

If I thought I might need *ten* orchestrations, I would have had them prepared, because that's my nature. I wanted this right, not right if, not right maybe, not right unless. I wanted this as right as Barbra wanted it. I wanted to please her, but I also wanted to please myself. And so plan "B" it was, and we never looked back.

For all the times a composer is turned down by a singer, for all the times a composer doesn't get his first choice of vocalists, for all the frustrations that come with the territory—and I know that the lows can be very low—this high made up for all of them.

We were done. I found myself on Sunset Boulevard outside the recording studio at 2:30 A.M. I was exhilarated. The tape of "The Way We Were" was burning a hole in my pocket. I was anxious to share the great news; I had to tell someone. But who? I felt like an atheist who's won the lottery and doesn't know who to thank.

It's 2:30 A.M. That means it's 5:30 A.M. in New York. I certainly don't want to wake up my parents or my sister. It's 10:30 A.M. in London, but I don't know anybody in London. I don't know too many people at all. I mean, I'd been wearing blinders during these years, and I hadn't let anyone or anything get me off the track.

Call me obsessed with work, but after all, it had gotten me this far.

I remember the night of the first preview of *The Way We Were*. In the movie's final sequence, Streisand meets Redford years after their marriage has come unglued. He has gone back to his affluent life, she to her life of rebellion and radicalism. She is outside the Plaza Hotel, agitating to ban the bomb, when she sees him, his beautiful new girlfriend on his arm. He moves toward her. Barbra touches that unruly lock on his forehead. Katie still adores the Adonis.

Now the Hamlisch acid test for movie emotion is simple: Do people cry? The audience at the preview had not, and I knew part of the blame was mine. I had specifically shied away from using "The Way We Were" music in this final scene, because I thought it would be excessive. Leo Shuken, my arranger, had disagreed: "Marvin, if you play it twenty times, the audience may think they've only heard it three or four times. Remember, while *you* are listening to the clarinet and the oboe, *they* are listening to the dialogue." He was right. I knew now without a doubt that the theme had to be there at the end. This would push the audience over the edge into tears.

I tried to convince the head of Columbia's music department to spend the money to call another session. It would take fifty-five musicians to add this bit of music to the last ninety seconds of the film. The studio would have to pay the union musicians for three hours' work. I had come this far, and yet I felt as if I had been assembling a four-hundred-piece jigsaw puzzle and had suddenly found that the last piece was missing. I was willing to wager anything to make it clear how vital this piece really was, not just to me but to the picture. I was terrified that Columbia Pictures would turn me down.

What happens if they say no?

My apprehensions were well founded. After hearing me out, the music department chief snapped: "Kid—we're not spending one extra penny on rerecording." But I knew it had to be done. And somehow I'd see to it. Sometimes you have to put your money where your heart is. Sometimes I know what I need to do, and rational thought gives way to high-strung emotion. This picture had everything going for it, and I wasn't going to sit by and let it slip away for a mere ninety seconds. So I went back to the head of the music department and told him that I'd pay for the rerecording myself.

I'm not sure if he believed me. But he said if I'd do that, he would let me go ahead. (Frankly, I was hoping he would say: "Hey, kid, if you feel like that, hell, we'll pay for it. Plus we'll give you a hefty bonus." But this wasn't a movie; this was the movie business.)

So I spent the money, which, believe me, wasn't mere pocket change.

And the new music went into the movie. Finally, I had exactly what I wanted.

I waited for the next preview.

Streisand sees Redford with his new girlfriend outside the Plaza. She touches his unruly lock of hair. And then the music builds and sweeps the screen.

I was standing at the back of the movie house; I heard a woman start to cry. And then I heard another. And within minutes, there wasn't a dry eye left.

I knew I was right. And knowing it was right made it worth every penny. I don't know why I get this way. I don't know why I can't stop until I know everything is the way it ought to be.

While *The Way We Were* was in postproduction, I got a message from director George Roy Hill. I had loved his *Butch Cassidy and the Sundance Kid*, and he said he needed to talk to me right away.

"Marvin, it's not an original score I need. All I want you to do is adapt some music for me."

I was reminded of what I had told Sam Spiegel's secretary when she phoned and asked me to play the piano at his party. "Please . . . I'm a college student. I'm a Juilliard man. . . . I do not play parties." What I told Hill was "Please, I don't do adaptations. I'm a composer. I write my own music." But once again I heeded the biblical injunction that pride goeth before a fall.

I agreed to see a first cut in the screening room. I quickly realized that this was one of the best pictures I had seen in years. I loved this tale of a pair of con men, Paul Newman and Robert Redford, who set out to put the "sting" on a big-city racketeer and do so in a most ingenious way. David Ward had written a witty, stylish script, George Roy Hill had directed it faultlessly, and Newman and Redford were the best screen couple in years.

From the beginning, George Roy Hill's idea had always been to use the ragtime music of Scott Joplin. Though I was not exactly a Joplin aficionado, I loved the sound of honky-tonk music for this movie. One of the things that drew me to *The Sting* was that George had been shrewd enough to leave little oases without dialogue for the music. He built montages and sequences into the picture for this purpose. Whenever I see patches in a film that are talkless, I'm in heaven. For it is in these celestial spaces that the man who does the music can spread his wings and be *heard.* Some of the greatest themes you've ever heard, from "Lara's Theme" to the "Pink Panther," are in those segments that are empty of dialogue. George Roy Hill had provided Burt Bacharach with one such sequence in *Butch Cassidy and the Sundance Kid*, the bicycle-riding montage, and Bacharach repaid him with "Raindrops Keep Fallin' on My Head."

I was well aware that there were other musicians who knew the music of Scott Joplin far more intimately than I, men who had popularized Joplin's famous piano "rags." But the truth is, none of them had experience in the movies. I knew how to write for film, marrying music to the length of each scene, and I could also play the piano "rags"—those Juilliard piano lessons were about to pay off. George had chosen some pieces from the world of Scott Joplin that he wanted to use in the film. I examined the entire Joplin library and chose my favorites.

In five days flat the job was done. That's right, George. I've never told you that. In five days it was over. Writing an original theme for a film takes time, but that was not the job here. Instead, I chose from preexisting material, and that was much easier. I quickly figured out what went where, adapted the music, timed it, cut it up, and the rest was history. I phoned my agent and said those words that had become a leitmotif of my life:

"I'm finished. What do I do now?"

"Whatever you do," he said, "don't tell them you've finished in five days. Call them in three weeks and tell them it's coming along nicely."

Which is what I did.

George Roy Hill was what every director should be for a composer. If I told him I had a problem and needed a little more time in a scene to accommodate the music—or a little less—he would try to make the adjustment. He also would ask my opinion about certain scenes in the movie and how they played. That's a rare collaborator. Until George Roy Hill, no one had ever asked my opinion of anything on which I was working. Believe it or not, directors only wanted to know if I could write the music and how long it would take. You'd think they'd want to know what I honestly thought of the film. But composer, beware. As Sam Goldwyn once told an underling, "I don't like yes men, so give me your honest opinion, even if it costs you your job."

The real fun came for me when we started recording the soundtrack. We didn't have a full-size orchestra, as with *The Way We Were*, but we had eight or nine great musicians, with yours truly at the keyboard. We spent hours making ragtime; the piano player in me had found a long-lost brother in Scott Joplin.

Having recorded the score for *The Way We Were* and *The*

Sting, I needed no gift of clairvoyance to know that they'd capture plenty of attention. I also knew that these two films had tapped into my best work, and I was clamoring for what I had done to be heard. But no such luck. There I was, Marvin Hamlisch, trying to be disciplined and behave himself for once. It's called "waiting patiently." It's never been my strongest suit.

Finally, thank heaven, the two films were released within months of each other and were huge hits. The music for *The Sting* was getting a lot of mention in the reviews. (Who would have guessed that a ragtime single would bounce to the top of the charts?) Of course, there were critics. Some carped that Scott Joplin's music was out of place in a movie set in another era. The film was set in the thirties; the Joplin "rags" were written around the turn of the century. I had been aware of this. I knew this might cause a problem for some purists. But the music and movie had a great kinship—a good humor and high spirits. "If I thought a jazz band would give me the feeling I wanted for a Roman epic," George Roy Hill said, "I'd use it." *And I'd write it.*

With these two films, I had done a musical adaptation, composed a score, and written a theme song all in one year. As for "The Way We Were," let's face it, with Barbra Streisand to sing it, it couldn't miss—it became her first number 1 hit song.

Well, I'd be lying to you if I told you that it didn't cross my mind, fairly quickly, what the three music categories of the Academy of Motion Picture Arts and Sciences were: Best Song in a motion picture, Best Adaptation for a motion picture, Best Score for a motion picture. I figured I had a reasonable crack at at least *one* nomination.

I figured right, but my arithmetic was bad.

I was nominated in all *three* categories.

* * *

Just prior to Oscar night, there is a party given for the nominees. The party is really a chance for the press to meet and talk with the stars. There were no fistfights among the reporters struggling to get at the composers. However, one newspaper woman for the *Cleveland Plain-Dealer* approached me with a sage observation and a bit of advice.

"You know, Marvin," she said, "when we write our stories on the Academy Awards, we hardly ever mention the people who win for music. We only write about the top five—Best Picture, Best Actor, Best Actress, Best Supporting Players. It's very rare that we mention anyone else. So if you win and you're not in one of those five categories, you have to say something pretty unique to get press attention."

Hmm. I thought about what she said. Maybe this would work: "When I came to Hollywood I had nothing but seven dollars and my brother's high-heeled shoes. But I had a song in my heart." Maybe not.

I decided not to dwell on it. It wasn't customary for composers to get much recognition from winning an Oscar. Composers just aren't news. It reminded me of the time my press agent asked a reporter from the *Los Angeles Times*, "How do I get Marvin's name in your newspaper?" and he replied, "Shoot him."

I'm not by nature superstitious, but as I looked at the tux I had worn the night I lost for *Kotch*, I decided to go for the big bucks and buy a new one. Why take chances? I sent my parents airline tickets for the gala night, although my mother, ever frugal, wondered if I should spend this kind of money.

"Marvin, it's crazy to spend so much. We can watch you at home. When you lose, think of the money you'll have saved."

But I insisted and told them I wanted them there, no matter what. And so they came out, and on April 2, 1974, my parents, my sister, and my dear friend Liza Minnelli went off with me to the Oscars at the Dorothy Chandler Pavilion.

Liza was my buddy that evening, calming me down as I sat through one award after another. It felt as if I had been sitting there since my bar mitzvah.

The first music award was in the Adaptation category.

"And the winner is Marvin Hamlisch."

I raced to the stage. But this time, I told myself, "Marvin, this is not the Golden Globes. This is the Oscars. Say thank you, be brief, and get the hell off."

I took my own advice. Of course, I was thrilled to win an Oscar. What better measure of success in the film industry? My parents were beaming. I remember the big hug I got from Liza when I was ushered back to my seat. We couldn't help but remember that Christmas night and that first demo record. Liza had won her Oscar just a year earlier for *Cabaret*.

From then on things became a bit of a blur, but I have to confess that one thing was clear in my mind: typical Marvin Hamlisch. It wasn't that I was ungrateful and that the Oscar didn't please me, but I started feeling that winning for adapting a score from Scott Joplin's music wasn't "quite in the same league" as winning an Oscar for music I had written myself.

By now the blur became a whirlwind:

"The envelope, please."

"And the winner is *The Way We Were*, original score by Marvin Hamlisch."

I made my second trip up the aisle, I was handed the Oscar, thanked the producer and the director, and did my thank-yous. This time I was collected enough not to forget to thank the makers of Maalox.

I was ushered backstage, surrounded by well-wishers and the press. I guess if you get two Oscars, composers *do* get attention from the press. Questions were coming from all directions. I was blinded by flashbulbs. There was so much noise and commotion backstage that I lost track of what was happening out front. I was in mid-sentence with some interviewer when I suddenly heard the unmistakable "The Way We Were" wafting backstage from the orchestra—and I realized that I had won the Oscar for Best Song of the year.

I ran out onto the stage. This was getting even too wild for me. I kissed Alan and Marilyn, we all thanked Barbra Streisand, Columbia Pictures, Ray Stark, Redford, our agents, and the cast and crew. I caught a glimpse of my parents, Liza, my sister. I was dazed. As I looked out at the audience, the faces had become familiar to me by now. I blurted out: "I think we can now talk as friends. . . ."

My career in movie music had all come together with these two big box-office smash hits. Suddenly, I was on Johnny Carson, Merv Griffin, and Mike Douglas. I showed America that a composer did not have to live in a garret with no heat, a crust of bread, and some cheap wine. You know the scene: Puccini, *La Bohème*, act 1. What people were also finding out was that I could be funny, a bit zany, and that I could talk to people other than violinists. I was being asked back.

But Oscar night also bore some sour fruit. I received a raft of angry letters declaring that Scott Joplin deserved the award for *The Sting*, not me. I knew better than to think that I was going to rip off Scott Joplin. I knew full well that on this film I was doing an adaptation. Joplin had written the music. But the Oscar for Adaptation is given to the person who does the adapting, not the composing. Scott Joplin, whether born in the nineteenth century or today, had written his music with no intention of using it in a movie. Suddenly, another musician (me) comes along and uses it in a film. Once that happens, if the Academy feels the adaptation is worthy of an award, then the adapter, not the composer, receives it. I answered every one of the letters, explaining the rules of the Academy.

For better or worse, TV was making me an instant celebrity. People were recognizing me on the street. Oddly enough, I can't say they told me how much they loved my music, but they kept telling me how much they loved my sense of humor. I remember one strange, unexpected voice. It startled me:

"So, Marvin, isn't it time to go back to writing music? Johnny Carson will get along without you just fine." I didn't have to turn around to see who it was. It was the voice of my father in my head, and it resonated loudly.

There were other warnings. A few months after the Oscar ceremony, I was at a party at which someone said something to me that was on a par with "Beware the ides of March." He was a movie director with whom my sister, Terry Liebling (by now a well-known casting director), had worked. This man said something that proved to be prescient and profound. He pulled a long face not in keeping with the occasion and said:

"You know, Marvin, it's too bad you got this so young."

Come on, I thought. This guy has got to be kidding. I had won three Oscars in one night. There couldn't possibly be a cloudy sky behind that rainbow. But my private Cassandra knew something that I didn't. Or did I? This man had said something that I had considered myself. My inner voice had warned me that by winning big at age twenty-nine I was violating some sort of natural law.

This fellow's warning also triggered something else and more important inside of me. He was right. I had been obsessed with my career, with putting myself on the map. Well, I was there, and the chase was over. Yet until now I had never wondered where all this was leading. To someone young and impetuous, personal happiness was equated with success. To become a celebrity was to become *ipso facto* happy, and it started becoming clear to me what was missing. I was lonely.

Whatever there was of a personal life was inextricably entwined with my professional life. It was as though my two hands were tied together, so wherever my right one (my professional life) had gone, my left (my personal life) followed. To my way of thinking, winning the Academy Awards was the only ticket I needed for personal happiness. But I now heard, over and over and over again, "Marvin, it's too bad you got this so young."

It made me think about that Oscar night. Liza Minnelli was my date that evening, but she's a friend, not a sweetheart. She went to her house, and I went to my apartment. It was a thrilling night, but now it was over and I was alone.

Three Oscars under your arm and you come home and empty the cat litter.

8.

NOTES FROM *A CHORUS LINE*

PART I

May 3, 1974

Michael Bennett called. "Marvin, I know you're probably stuck in Hollywood now, but drop everything and come to New York."

I told him yes.

May 7, 1974

It's extraordinary to me that the big decisions are made in seconds. I returned the Hertz car and said good-bye to the apartment on La Cienega and Fountain. Made the dreaded call to my motion-picture agent. Gave him the bad news. He can't believe that I'm crazy enough to abandon Hollywood after the three Oscars. "Marvin," he asks me, "are you nuts?" (Finally, he's noticed.) I knew I had let him down.

I flew back to New York. No Valium this time. It feels great to be back—land of Juilliard, Miss Sussman, and my mother's veal cutlets. Who says you can't go home again?

May 8, 1974

Early afternoon. I'm on my way to see Michael at his apartment on West Fifty-fifth Street. I know this guy's going to be the next Jerome Robbins. He was brilliant with *Company* and *Follies*. What Michael is, is a visionary, an extraordinary mixture of energy and ideas. I still can't forget his choreography for *A Joyful Noise*. If there's anyone to break the mold of the American musical, it's Michael Bennett. That's not to say he isn't ultratheatrical, overconfident, and, at times, very arrogant.

The apartment is painted all in black with recessed spotlights. Tony awards all precisely in a row. Understatement is obviously not one of Michael's qualities.

He's still got that trim beard, short, short hair. He continues to let me dangle, and then he springs it on me.

"It's about dancers."

I'm not sure what reaction he expected, if any.

"I have these stories about dancers. I taped them. They talked to me about their lives. It was like an evening of group therapy. These ever-smiling chorus kids who spend their lives backing up the star in return for peanuts and bruised patellas. Pretty soon, they just poured out their souls to me. They talked about their childhood, their agony with their families, the problems of sex, being straight, being gay, their struggles in the business, all of it. And I've got it all on tape."

He started circling me with his catlike walk. It's Michael being theatrical even at home, taking control.

He hit his stride.

"No stars, no sets, just dancers. Marvin this is gonna be way out on a limb. We're gonna show 'em. Joe Papp's already given us seed money." He was oddly wild about this.

Obviously, I must've missed something. He flashed that little grin of his that says: I'm way ahead of you.

I came here for this?

May 9, 1974

I decided to walk home. I needed time to get out of the dark. (Black walls do that to you every time.) Where's the plot, where's the story, where's the music?

I keep hearing Michael in my head. The intensity of his voice. It was his confidence that started to envelop me. I realized that another talent of his was the ability to persuade. I'm beginning to sense there's a bandwagon here. I better get on it now. I'll figure out where it's going later.

If M.B. is going to extend the boundaries of Broadway and change its form, then here's a chance for me to extend its musical horizons.

"So, Marvin, tell us," my mother asked, "what did Michael have to say for himself?"

"What's the show about?" my father joined in.

What could I tell them?

"It's about dancers," I said rather meekly. I tried to say more, but truthfully, that's all I really knew.

The silence was finally broken when my mother asked: "A show about dancers? So, do you want celery in your tuna fish sandwich or not?"

I made the decision to put my money on Michael. There would be no second-guessing on my part. I also made the decision that it was time to get my own apartment. Living at home had been very beneficial. The food was great, and the price was right, but I was twenty-nine years old.

I was thrilled to find a small one-bedroom apartment on East Seventy-ninth Street. I couldn't believe it was on Park Avenue. When I saw what it would cost, I knew it was on Park Avenue. It was already furnished; in fact, it was a designer apartment in this spanking new building. What could be better? No furniture to buy, no decorator to hire, no swatches, no paint chips. And there was even room service. More important, they assured me they had absolutely no objections to a piano. (Drums were another story.)

They made sure to let me know the apartment was done by Jay Spectre. (I had no idea who that was until someone told me he was a prominent decorator.) From then on, I got a kick out of telling people that Jay Spectre had done the apartment especially for me. Hey, why not?

One week after I signed the lease, I moved in.

May 12, 1974

The movers brought the piano today. I'm eating on paper plates and paper cups. It saves me from having to wash dishes and glasses. But tonight turns into a night from hell. I started playing the Yamaha upright to hear what it sounds like. The next thing I know, the concierge is on the phone telling me there were complaints about the noise. Mrs. Vandertusch is quite upset. She has a very nervous dog.

Of course, if Beethoven, in his later years, had lived here, he wouldn't have had any problem. He wouldn't have *heard* the concierge.

May 15, 1974

I can't believe I have to move outta here. Back to my mother's house? No way. I've just gotta solve this noise problem.

I called a carpenter. He said he'd come tomorrow. He says he can do something to deaden the sound of the piano.

May 16, 1974

The carpenter showed up today. He checked the floor and the walls and tells me there's only one solution. "Mr. Hamliste," (they always have trouble with that name) "I have to build a soundproof box around the piano."

May 20, 1974

I can't believe what's going on. I've watched these guys take four days to build a wooden insulated box around the piano. Three Oscars and I have to go through this? I'm genuinely thrilled for my neighbors. They can't hear any music when I play. The trouble is, neither can I. It all sounds like the piano is in Budapest. That's how soft it's coming out. The piano is three inches off the ground. I am very uncomfortable.

May 21, 1974

Michael wants me to call Ed Kleban. He's already picked him to do the lyrics for the show. Michael has heard some of his stuff and says he's the next Sondheim. Ed's already listened to the tapes.

May 23, 1974

I finally got Ed on the phone. We arranged to meet tomorrow. He told me not to call between noon and three because he doesn't answer his calls. *He must get his afternoon nap.* (What luck. I'm working with a narcoleptic.)

Because the box had to be painted today, we decided to meet at my parents' apartment. Time for more veal cutlets.

May 24, 1974

My first impression of Ed is that he is very intellectual, methodical, quiet, and a genuinely nice guy. Just meeting him today has made this project seem more of a reality. Having listened to all the tapes, he filled me in on his ideas. We'll meet again in a few days.

He suggested we use his place. He can play his piano late into the night without worrying about the neighbors. Only trouble is, Ed's having trouble with his air conditioner. Do I want to be in Budapest or a steam bath?

May 25, 1974

Today was the first real talk I had with Ed about the show. One of the dancers, Nick Dante, has transcribed the tapes, and I have now read most of them. Michael has decided that Nick will do the script. To be candid, I'm a bit uneasy about this. Nick was a dancer and has no experience as a book writer.

Ed and I discussed the open, honest, confessional nature of the material. *Now the problem is how to make a musical out of all this.* We're not even sure Michael knows.

But my creative juices are bubbling. I'm starting to hear

things. Whatever this show needs, it isn't conventional songs. I know I want it all to sound as if the music and the stories are totally "seamless."

June 6, 1974

Today Michael startled us when he said he saw the show coming out of a series of workshops. The plan is to rehearse four, five, or six weeks in a rehearsal studio, then shut down completely and see what's evolved. "Nobody is going to rush this project. If we like it, we'll do another workshop," he says. I guess this will go on until we're ready. I'm still not sure what I think about all this.

I had come to New York in a big hurry, and now Michael and his workshop idea were starting to slow me down. I felt frustrated. Where was the pressure? Marvin Hamlisch without sixteen projects, three bottles of Maalox, and with free time was getting to me. I had to make a major adjustment in the way I did things. I was used to coming into a project and writing everything I had to write to deadline. Now there was to be no fixed time frame.

Shows used to go out of town, play a few weeks, make changes, and then come into New York. Creators of these shows always complained that there was never enough time to fix things. Deadlines for musicals had proven to be "deadly." So, Michael reasoned, why not rehearse in New York for as long as it took, until we got it right?

I had to alter the way I thought about things. Perhaps learning to slow down would suit me, give me time to think for a change. We were all young: Michael was thirty-one, Ed was thirty-five, Nick was thirty-three, and I was thirty. All rebels eager to set Broadway on its ear.

June 12, 1974

Michael decided to hold open auditions for the first workshop, which will start in August. It never occurred to me that he wasn't going to use the people he already had on tape for the show. The tapes were just an experiment. Tons of people showed up. It seems as though everyone wants to be in a M.B. show.

June 21, 1974

Our "script" for now consists of Nick's transcriptions. Michael has picked what he thinks are the best stories. I'm not so sure I agree. I heard them read at auditions. Some sounded emotional; many others were duds.

Ed and I are now going to intensify our sessions to figure out what to musicalize. I take the transcripts home and spread them out on the living-room carpet. Slowly, I choose the stories that would musicalize best and the ideas I feel are the most intriguing about each character. I also want to make sure there is enough variety in the characters.

The more I listen to the tapes, the more I have been struck with the spontaneity of the kids. The songs must be absolutely lifelike. They must sound like true stories, as if they're coming from the dancers' hearts and minds. But how?

If we can make this work, it would all be so staggering.

August 14, 1974

What a hell of a few weeks it's been. The two of us haven't written much. Ed smokes. My apartment always smells like a Vegas lounge. I bought a No Smoking sign and put it next to the chair he uses. I doubt I will sleep tonight. It's already 2:00 A.M.

Tomorrow we start our first day of workshop. I think of us as Michael's Merry Men, ready to follow him into Sherwood Forest. I can't wait to see Michael working on his feet. I know that's when this will all come together.

August 15, 1974

By now Michael sees *the entire show* set at an audition. I like this. I like the way he takes things to extremes. I can't fall into any old-fashioned musical traps. So far, Michael has been very supportive. I can't explain it. There's something magical between us. I'm tired, trying to figure out what we've got here, and loving every minute of this craziness. I'm on my way to Broadway, and this is what I've wanted all my life.

August 18, 1974

Michael may have arranged my "professional marriage" to Ed, but I wish we had more courting time. We are very different.

I'm "up." He's quiet, silent sometimes. He came over with tons of yellow legal pads. He's obsessed with knowing everything he can about the dancers. Without this, he says, he can't write a lyric. And I need a title or a lyric idea to get me going.

Ed would have made a great researcher for Martin Gilbert when he wrote his *Second World War: A Complete History*. But with Ed, Gilbert would have quit after Poland.

But I love Ed. He is so damned smart. Sometimes he even makes me laugh. I wish we had a picture of the way we work. Here we are, in the same room, with a piano in a box. He's smoking and napping and writing; I'm coughing and composing. Not a pretty picture, I confess.

August 20, 1974

Ed said to me today: "The main all-consuming thing about these dancers is how endlessly desperate they are for work. The job is the Holy Grail." And then he handed me a yellow piece of paper from his pad. There were only four simple lines on it:

God I hope I get it
I really need this job
Oh God I need this job
Please help me get this job

In these simple words, Ed has caught the essence of what our show is about. You might say the music and lyrics were born at this moment. I had all I needed. It was time for me to crawl into the box.

August 24, 1974

With the opening done, Ed and I pick up speed. We write two more songs real quick. One is called "I Can Do That," about a dancer first discovering his talent. The other is called "At the Ballet," which is about the endless years of training dancers endure. We played it for M.B., and he said it was perfect. I love getting praise from someone who matters to me. I had thoughts of Miss Goldstein.

I went out for a coffee ice cream sundae. I deserve it.

August 30, 1974

Suddenly, I'm starting to get worried. There's a great new danger here. *This whole thing could get boring.* Michael seems to be losing sight of what he set out to do in the first place: to probe as deeply as did the tapes. Michael is getting carried away. He's losing focus. His instincts as a choreographer are turning this into a showcase for dancers.

Michael keeps asking me to write dance numbers. If we're not careful, we could lose the human element. We could end up with a string of fifteen songs about dancers, and not people. We could end up with a sameness that would sink us. I remind Michael of his original idea: These people have to live real lives as real people.

M.B. hears me out but dismisses what I have to say. I go home and fix some instant oatmeal—the one meal I've perfected in my Jay Spectre apartment.

September 7, 1974

Final week of first workshop. To be fair, I've seen Michael brilliant most of the time, but I've also seen him be the control freak. When he doesn't get his way, get out of the way. He shouts and behaves terribly. We're all still trying to find this show. I know it's there. There's no doubt it's there.

Michael wants a run-through even though we only have a few songs and way too much dialogue. It lasted almost four hours. Michael asked me what I thought. "I think it's a trifle long," I joked, "and a little wordy." But what worked, worked.

September 18, 1974

Michael called a meeting. The run-through was an eye-opener. Michael sees what's wrong and instantly knows what has to be done. What a great squadron leader he would have made for a kamikaze outfit.

He listens to all our ideas. He still hasn't given up the idea of more dance numbers. Yet it's clear that we all have the same goal: to turn the American musical on its head and do something innovative and explosive. So what else is new?

We all agree that there are too many subplots. The dialogue is all tangled. There's too much of it.

November 15, 1974

I'm determined to write character songs, not dance numbers. Ed and I did a song about one of the dancers in acting class who struggled and struggled but who never impressed her teacher. He hated her work.

When he told her to see how it felt to be an ice cream cone, she said, "I felt nothing." When he told her to see how it felt to ride a bobsled, she said, "I felt nothing." Then the song continues:

Six months later I heard that
Karp had died.
And I dug right down to the bottom
of my soul and cried.
'Cause I felt . . . nothing.

Another song we've almost got is a howler. I hope we can get away with it. It's about this ultratalented, skinny dancer who never seems to get a job and can't figure out why. One day, lightning strikes. Her dancing is always a ten; her looks are always a three. She finally gets the message on what show business is all about. Boobs and buns.

"That's easy," she figures. "I can buy 'em. There're plastic surgeons all over this town." She'll show 'em. At her next audition, her dancing is ten, and her looks are ten. Money well spent. Not only that; Ed and I think we've got our showstopper for sure: "Tits and Ass."

November 18, 1974

These last two songs convince me that our show is working. Michael loves them and loves the slant we're taking.

I truly feel that my whole life's work has been a preparation for this show. I seem at home doing this kind of work. I'm not trying to write hits or hummable songs. I just keep trying to sound spontaneous.

Out of the blue, Michael calls. He says it's very important. He wants another dance number. I tell him he's dead wrong. He insists. I tell him he's dead wrong again. I won't do it.

November 20, 1974

Michael has just fired me. He went bananas when I told him he was wrong. I disobeyed an order from Herr Bennett.

I immediately called my manager, Allan Carr, who flew in from Los Angeles to set up a meeting with Michael. Ed called to let me know that Michael told him what had happened. I was sure Ed would hold firm, that he would tell Michael that without me he was leaving. But that only happens in the movies. In real life, it goes this way: Since he also wrote music, Ed said he was ready to finish the score by himself.

Allan has set up a meeting for me and Michael in two days. I told Allan I would do everything I could to make the meeting go well but that I did not want Michael to think I was his rubber stamp.

When we met, I told Michael I would not endorse an idea that I genuinely felt would damage the show. He had to trust me. Any more numbers about dancing would make this an "insider" show.

"Michael," I said, "I want to make sure that your vision—of empathy with the lives of these dancers as people—stays up there as strongly as possible."

He kept saying, "We can pull this off, you know. We really can. Let me think it over." And then he hugged me. Michael and I really love each other.

I sensed my point had hit home, but with Michael Bennett, there are no guarantees.

January 24, 1975

We just started the second workshop. The battle with Michael is behind me. He's real fast on staging. His genius is making things work and come alive. His sense of the theatrical is unmatchable. He's also street-smart, and his reaction time is like lightning when his feet hit the stage. It's spellbinding to watch him.

But dialogue, on the other hand, is a different story. Michael takes forever to make cuts. For him to take out thirty seconds is like eight-hour brain surgery, even though the final incision leaves the patient better than before.

January 29, 1975

The show needs some sort of summing up. Michael and I feel it must come in a slow, haunting song. So I stroll through Central Park. Where else can you find inspiration in this town? But it's freezing out there. So I hopped on the crosstown bus. And wouldn't you know, a melody slipped into my head on

Seventy-ninth Street between Fifth and Madison. It stayed with me for hours. I played it for Ed. He thinks it's right.

February 2, 1975

I'm working on the melody. Maybe I should get back on the bus. The tune can't be overly sentimental. Yet it must answer the paramount question of the evening: If these dancers had to stop dancing forever, would they still think it had all been worth it?

The answer is an emphatic yes. What these kids had done, they had done for love. And that was the lyric Ed came up with. It's masterful and emotional and, in its own way, heartbreaking. "What I Did for Love" says it all.

February 8, 1975

Up until now the stage was bare. There has been no definition of space. The atmosphere has been relaxed. Michael did something today that has had a profound effect on the show and on me.

He drew a white line on the floor, and in that simple act was the epitome of Michael's genius. He galvanized everyone. There was a whole new feeling. Everything took on a depth and meaning that had not quite been there before.

What he did was symbolize the show in one fell swoop. For *A Chorus Line* is all about being on the line, all of us, auditioning all the time.

February 10, 1975

The decision has been made to open off-Broadway, at Joe Papp's Public Theatre. We are scheduled to go into full-fledged rehearsal on March 5. A budget has been drafted.

Michael has new thoughts about the finale. He wants a celebration of a chorus line. Suddenly, he sees the need for costumes. And not just costumes. Expensive, gorgeous, gold costumes. He wants the cast—who till now have worn rehearsal clothes, sweat socks and leotards, tights and leg warmers—to miraculously change into gold and spangles.

The dancers are gonna go high-kicking their way through the glorious final dance combination—pyrotechnical and spectacular. The chorus kids, who normally do a number like this behind the star, will now take center stage and become the star themselves.

I love this idea. These dancers have become one.

February 11, 1975

Ed rushes over (no nap today) and hands me a crumpled piece of yellow paper from one of his infamous pads. All I see is:

One singular sensation,
Every little step she takes.
One thrilling combination,
Every move that she makes.

The Rockettes flashed in front of my eyes. The key to the whole thing is that after the word "One," I needed to make room for a real old-fashioned chorus-line kick. And that did it. Once I had that, the song practically writes itself.

February 23, 1975

Had a great run-through. The staging of "One" is brilliant. Michael is definitely right about the gold and spangles. The audience will go out of the theatre screaming.

Just one problem. Joe Papp says we can't have the costumes. "Boys," he said, "we've run out of money."

PART II

Michael set up a meeting with the Shubert Organization for additional financing.

"Now Marvin, don't give them any of the esoteric songs. Just play 'Tits and Ass,' 'Nothing,' and 'One.' We're here to raise money, not to raise their consciousness. When we get what we want, we'll let 'em hear the ballad."

"Tits and Ass" was a logical choice to open with. We knew it would have them in the palm of our hands. This song by itself was hot enough to get us the backing. The Shubert offices had a piano that must have been a hundred years old, a real vintage thing. Rudolf Friml probably played "Indian Love Call" on this baby. I was sure no one had played this piano in at least fifty years. It was more a decorative piece, to be looked at but not touched.

We're there trying to make a good impression. After all, we needed to get $200,000 from these people. So after Michael set the scene for the song I was to play, I crossed to the piano and opened the dusty lid. Michael said, "Hit it, kid," and I did. I played the opening chord—a *bam* in B-flat minor.

And the piano collapses.

It falls with an enormous crash. It's been sitting on legs that were broken years before, perhaps in some scuffle over the score for *Good News*. It had been propped up like that for half a century. Now you see some very sensitive artists doing some very heavy lifting. Michael, Ed, set designer Robin Wagner, and I are all trying to lift that damn piano back onto its feet so we can get on with the audition, because we really need those costumes. And we're trying to play it very cool, like pianos collapse on us every day.

So the wandering minstrels finally get on with the audition, and they loved it, and that is how the Shuberts, Bernie Jacobs and Jerry Schoenfeld, bless them, got involved in the show. They came up with the $200,000, and Michael got his top hats and spangles.

What we learned from the success of "Tits and Ass" was that *A Chorus Line* still needed some more laughs—and quick. Here comes a piece of Michael's craftiness. He knew that Nick Dante had no flair for comedy, and this was no time for any risks. So, unbeknownst to anyone, Michael trotted off to see his good friend Neil Simon: "Neil, we have to keep this between us, but I need your help. We need more laughs." Neil Simon smiled. Laughs, he thought. Michael handed him the script, and he started scribbling at a furious pace. And presto, Michael had exactly what he came for.

Now the plot thickens. At the next rehearsal, Michael arrived with a sheet of paper tucked in his pocket, and miraculously—whenever a joke was needed—like a rabbit out of a hat, Michael would go to his list and come up with a humdinger. This happened time and time again. By now I knew Michael pretty well. And one thing I knew for sure is that he was no comedian. So all of us are sitting there dazzled and wondering how the hell, out of nowhere, he's become the next Neil Simon. We couldn't believe how, overnight, he had become so deliciously witty. None of us thought at the time to wonder where that piece of paper had come from. So, belatedly, thank you very much, Neil.

Suddenly, the show had all come together. The four-hour monster had become a two-hour musical. I was confident of the music now, for it was freewheeling and had captured the stories of the dancers' lives. Ed's lyrics were stunning, combining intelligence, wit, and compassion. And, with some last-minute help from writer Jim Kirkwood, the book finally worked. I knew that the very best Michael Bennett could bring to a project he had brought to this one.

On April 16, 1975, we began previews down at the small Newman Theatre, with its bare brick walls and its four hundred seats. Right from the start there was a lot of positive buzz; the word was getting out among New York's theatre folk. It passed from the stage gypsies to the choreographers and directors and to the general public, whose antennae somehow pick up what's the upcoming show to look out for. It went even beyond that. We began to sense, which rarely happens in show business, that we were on the brink of a major breakthrough and about to succeed at creating a musical that would shatter the traditions of Broadway.

Even so, there were two problems that dogged us. One absolutely stupefied us. When we did "Tits and Ass" in rehearsal, it was instant hilarity. It was the song that hit the jackpot and got us $200,000. The only thing I can tell you is, mysteriously, at our first preview, the song died. I'm talking serious death. There was absolutely no audience response whatsoever, not a laugh, not a titter. (No, that might be the wrong word.) They just sat there. The same thing happened the second night, and then the third. Michael met Ed and me after the theatre had emptied:

"Guys, I have absolutely no idea why it's not working, but if it doesn't get a laugh soon, it's out. You'll just have to come up with another one."

"What?" I protested. "It's hysterical. It's funny. It worked a dozen times in rehearsal."

What was wrong with "Tits and Ass"? It was a puzzlement. That night I said to Ed, "I don't have the answer, but I know they're not seeing what we're seeing. So tomorrow night let's get to the theatre early, even have the ushers show us to our seats, and be in the audience from start to finish."

At the next evening's performance, we came through the front doors, were handed a program by an usher, and were escorted to our seats. Believe it or not, for the first time in four days, we actually saw a *Playbill*. We opened it and looked at the list of songs that were in the show.

And that's the magic moment when we realized our mistake.

"Tits and Ass" was there with all the others: "Tits and Ass." We had given away the game. They were in on the gag before Pam Blair sang a note. There was no surprise, no shock, no delight at the audacity of the song. The toothpaste was out of the tube.

Immediately, we changed the title of the song to "Dance, Ten; Looks, Three," the audition scores that had always plagued her. The new title didn't reveal a thing. All of a sudden the song worked, the audience howled, and it became a nightly showstopper. (Ultimately, the song came to be known as "Tits and Ass," anyway.)

The second problem we faced centered on the end of the show: Everything was building toward who gets a job in the chorus line and who doesn't. This was the ultimate moment of dramatic tension. The premise was that Zach, the character of the director in the show, started to single out dancers, one by one, and asked them to step forward: in the moment of silence that followed and in the smiles that broke out on these dancers' faces, it seemed certain they had indeed finally "gotten the job."

"Thank you very much," Zach says to them. But these words from a director at an audition are the kiss of death. These were actually the dancers who were sent home. The ones you thought were hired were actually the ones dismissed. The others standing in back had been picked for the chorus. Michael had been toying with that moment, fine-tuning it for a long time. It was a deft dramatic device; one could almost hear the audience gasp as the show ended in darkness. But leave it to Michael Bennett to come up with what probably remains the most ingenious curtain call in the history of the musical theatre.

I couldn't wait for opening night, but for some reason I was still worrying. I guess it wouldn't be me if I were calm and collected. But it was more than that. I had invested so much and worked for so long that I couldn't help wondering if we were right about what we had here. I guess I needed some kind of reassurance. I mean, after all this, there was no margin for error. It was as though my whole life would depend on those two hours once the houselights dimmed.

I was back on Maalox; I wasn't sleeping. I even grew uncharacteristically quiet. To put it succinctly, I was a mess. I went to see Michael, and we started talking.

"Michael," I asked, "what happens if we're wrong? What happens if the critics don't like it?"

He looked at me for a moment, and then with the savvy that was Michael Bennett, he said:

"Marvin, do you think you've done good work?"

"Yes."

"Do you love what you've done?"

"Yes."

"Do you think you wasted any of your time?"

"No."

"Then that's all you can do."

The show was frozen now. The previews continued to send the audience through the roof. The worst of it, though, was that there was nothing for me to do, which, as you know by now, is the Hamlisch curse. I got my "lucky tux" out of the closet, hailed a cab, and reached the theatre before any of the crowds had arrived. This was not going to be a Juilliard roof fiasco. I paced the lobby, then went backstage, hugged and kissed the kids in the cast, and gave each of them a special present.

"Five minutes, please."

"Places, please."

It was time to take my seat in the theatre, but in my peculiar crazy way, I knew I didn't have the stomach to sit through opening night. What I decided to do instead—believe it or not—was to go back home and sweat it out alone in my apartment. I did whatever I could do there to distract myself for about an hour and a half: went through the mail, put the dirty dishes in the washer, cleaned out the hall closet. Then, instinctively I knew it was time to hail a cab, go back down to the theatre, and arrive just at the start of the finale.

It was obvious that the performance had been phenomenal, and Michael's curtain call was indeed astonishing. Bedecked in golden costumes, dripping with spangles, and sporting sparkling top hats (let's hear it for $200,000 and a collapsed piano), the cast came on one at a time, taking their solo bows, and then hand in hand, formed a dazzling chorus line, kicking and strutting to the music of "One." The back wall was ablaze with mirror, reflecting not only the cast but the entire audience as well. The moment the kick line began, nothing short of pandemonium filled the theatre. It was a curtain call that captured the essence of the show and the essence of show business itself.

Like clockwork, the audience rose to its feet, and the ovation was thunderous. That we had a smash was clear. I had written the music exactly as I had wanted to. The audience saw the show exactly as I saw it. With this kind of sendoff, you'd have to be Marvin Hamlisch to think the reviews could be anything less than sensational. We went to Sardi's to wait for the morning papers. The reviews came in at about eleven o'clock. The New York Times Building is right next to Sardi's, and you can go outside and get the paper the second it comes out. So I rushed out to grab the paper, expecting the world to adore the show and love the music. Critic Clive Barnes called the show "tremendous." In the second paragraph, he called it "innovative" (by now, of course, I was wondering where his comments about the music were); in the third paragraph he called it "devastatingly effective"; in the fourth paragraph he talked about how simple this great idea really was. And on and on. And *then* came the paragraph about my music. I read each word very slowly.

> The music by Mr. Hamlisch is occasionally hummable. . . . Mr. Hamlisch is not such a good composer as he was in the movie "The Sting" when he was being helped out by Scott Joplin. . . .

I read it again just to make sure. My Juilliard stomach suddenly started acting up. This was the day, the night, the show, that I had always wanted, and now that that dream had arrived, it felt like a nightmare. I felt terrified and more vulnerable than ever before. Of course, this was only one review; there would be more. Michael and Joe Papp came over to me, and we went into another room in the restaurant. The situation quickly became all too clear as they read me the other reviews. The critics adored the show. They called it "brilliant," a "landmark for Broadway." There seemed to be only one problem with this musical—the music.

Joe Papp told me he was about to read the reviews to the cast. But he was going to delete the Hamlisch paragraphs. So there we were, everyone smiling and joking and celebrating, feasting on the expurgated version of the *New York Times* review. The cast also never got to hear what was said about me in the *Daily News*:

> Hamlisch has provided a score which [is] notably lacking in the least melodic or harmonic originality. . . .

By now I was dying—and throwing up. Just like in the old days.

The next day, there were lines around the block on Lafayette Street, crowds at the box office, people clamoring for the hottest ticket in town. And the composer was hiding in his apartment, experiencing the famous "Juilliard exam" feeling. I didn't want to set foot out of the house. I felt like Hester Prynne with the scarlet letter on her chest. I feared that if I walked down Columbus Avenue, people could read those reviews on my back. I knew that if I hailed a taxi, the driver would say, "Oh, no! You're the guy who wrote that music. Get yourself another cab."

I went into the throes of depression. It became a great effort for me to perform the simplest tasks, like walking or forking food into my mouth. My father talked to me. We were in my bedroom, and he told me honestly that I had written a very good score. I knew that he meant it. But I still wondered if shock treatment was legal in New York. Only my suicidal impulses led me to the corner newsstand. The world's greatest masochist was going to buy the afternoon paper, the *New York Post*, to read the inevitable slaughter by theatre critic Martin Gottfried.

I opened the paper slowly. I wandered around the sports section. Then I decided to check on the weather forecast for Honduras. I was jibbering by now and could barely believe it: "The best thing about [Hamlisch's] music," Gottfried said, "is that it is that rare animal, a theatre *score*. It isn't just a series of songs but an evening's worth of music designed to function as part of a stage work." But in my frenzied state I wasn't ready to believe a word of it. The show opened on a Wednesday. Thursday, Friday, and Saturday were like days without sunlight, and each day lasted about a month.

Then Sunday arrived—glorious, magnificent Sunday. On their front page, the *New York Times* reported that the last of the Apollo spacecraft had returned from space. But the big news for me was in the Arts and Leisure section. There was the Sunday review of *A Chorus Line* by that most highly esteemed of critics Walter Kerr. You know, the insightful, erudite, always on the mark, never-wrong Walter Kerr. In *his* review, Mr. Kerr declared that "the music was perfect." He talked at length about how I had captured the character of the dancers and really understood them.

The clouds lifted. I could go outside now. I could unashamedly tell people, "I'm the guy who wrote the music to *A Chorus Line*."

Of course, the music was never intended to stand out from the dialogue and the dancing. It was meant to be seamless. That was exactly what I aimed for all along. I wanted to be sure that the score acted as a kind of "train of thought." As each dancer began spilling out his or her innermost thoughts, the music would capture that abandon. Yes, certain songs might stand on their own, like "One" or "What I Did for Love," but for the most part, the score was intended to marry music to the flow of thoughts.

The *Chorus Line* experience was made so comfortable by Joe Papp, who trusted Michael and allowed the work to be done slowly, without pushing us for the final result. It was fortunate for us that Joe Papp was so forbearing, because anyone seeing *A Chorus Line* after the first workshop would have said, "Are you crazy?" Joe was patient, and he waited. When Michael told him it was ready, it was ready. The show had a miraculous run, moving to Broadway, garnering nine Tonys and the Pulitzer Prize, and became the longest-running American musical in history—fifteen years on Broadway, 6,238 performances. How I savor the memory of my first Broadway show. I wanted to get there so badly, and it all happened so perfectly. Putting together a creative team of writers who are all inspired by the same idea at the same time is a hell of a trick.

Years later, Michael called me with an idea for another innovative musical. I told him I would contact Ed and see what he thought. Michael was working on *Chess*, a London musical, at the time. We were scheduled to meet when he returned to New York in a couple of months. But Michael came back much earlier than that.

He had felt tired in London, so he flew home. He rested for a while, but when that didn't help, he saw a doctor. He learned he had AIDS. That was tragedy enough. And then Ed Kleban contracted tongue cancer. Soon they both were gone. A few years later, Nick Dante and Jimmy Kirkwood would be gone as well.

The creators of my beloved *Chorus Line*, those four singular sensations, have left us. It takes a lifetime to meet people of such gifts and to form such an unbreakable bond.

I won't forget / Can't regret / What we did for love.

9.

THEY'RE PLAYING OUR SONG

With *A Chorus Line* I had finally reached the place where I belonged—Broadway. I wanted to do more, and right away. It came as a blow that things don't work that way. There's a kind of emptiness when a show is over and your work is done, and with such a hit on my hands, I didn't expect it to take so long to fill the void. But there was no new *Chorus Line* waiting at my doorstep—I'd read dozens of scripts—not a single one that had any appeal or got my juices flowing again. The waiting seemed endless.

To have had such a triumph and then have nothing to follow it was terribly painful. I mean, it was wonderful to know that everyone was talking about *A Chorus Line* and singing those songs. I suppose it's what they mean by irony. I was a success now, and recognizable, but in truth I was living alone, and miserable without any work to do. So when an offer arrived to write the music for the James Bond thriller *The Spy Who Loved Me*, I grabbed it. I never really intended to go back to the movies, but when you're a Type A personality, work of any kind beats the emergency room at New York Hospital.

They wanted a hit title song, and they recommended the "hot new" lyricist in town: Carole Bayer Sager. We met in my apartment. She was terribly attractive: dark-haired; flashing eyes. She was quick, witty, hysterically funny, and fast. She took in the apartment, turned to me, and said: "I hope you don't think I'm prying, but I've worked with a lot of composers in my time, and I'm wondering: What the hell is your piano doing in a box?"

Lyrics poured out of her. She had a good ear for language and a head filled with ideas. The more we wrote together, the more time we spent together. We became inseparable. I was starting to get frightened. I began to wonder: Was it possible? Could I be having a professional and a private life at one and the same time? I figured out the answer to that question when Carole moved in. We lived and worked music. We constantly turned out new songs. Carole had brought me into the world of rock and roll. No sooner had we written "Nobody Does It Better," sung by Carly Simon, than it climbed to number 2 on the charts and was nominated for an Academy Award. We had more offers for films than we could handle now, and so we moved to California and started concentrating feverishly on song after song.

Although Carole seemed to thrive in Los Angeles, I felt somehow more and more that I was working against my better instincts, focusing on music that really wasn't very fulfilling. If there was one difficulty in being with Carole, I would say it came down to our being in different places musically. In retrospect, I should have pulled up stakes, gone back home, and turned every stone in New York to find another *Chorus Line*. But I couldn't bring myself to leave Carole, and by a twist of fate, if I wasn't going to get back east to Broadway, Broadway was going to come out west.

* * *

On a hot summer day in 1978, Neil Simon called. He had his sights set on turning his play *The Gingerbread Lady* into a Broadway musical. (An unlikely idea, but who was I to argue with Neil Simon?) He had already written hilarious books for the musicals *Sweet Charity*, *Little Me*, and *Promises, Promises.*

I met with Neil at his Bel-Air house to wrestle with *The Gingerbread Lady*. The lady put up quite a battle. But the nice part was that after each meeting I'd have Carole to return to, be with, and talk to. Then I'd go back for another meeting with Neil. In the old days, if someone like Neil Simon asked me, "How are you?," I'd answer, "Fine. Let's get to work." But nowadays I always had one topic on my mind: Carole. Being in a relationship was all new to me: "Can you believe it, Neil?" I'd say. "Last night Carole and I were about to go to this party when suddenly we get an idea for a song. I mean, we're dressed to go out, dinner jacket and evening gown, when we stop everything to write a song. Talk about not wasting a minute. . . ." Neil would smile wryly but tolerantly as I spun out my story. Then I'd tell him how Carole and I would always look to see whether my check from ASCAP or hers from BMI was larger. Neil would nod with amusement. And I'd go on about how Carole was into health food and that till we met, I didn't know the meaning of the word tofu. "Nowadays," I'd remark, "if I want a pastrami sandwich, I have to order out, since it's banned from the house." Neil would grin. Then we'd go back to *The Gingerbread Lady*.

It never dawned on me that my stories about the two of us had started the Simon creative juices flowing. I was puzzled when one day, a few months later, Carole and I received a brown envelope from Neil. I couldn't figure out what was in it, since by then he had abandoned *The Gingerbread Lady*. We found a typewritten manuscript inside. It was for an original musical Neil wanted us to read. I made my way through the first dozen or so pages and thought to myself, I must be dreaming. What was Neil up to? What was he trying to do to me? I confide in him, he listens, and then this: Neil Simon had written a musical about an award-winning Hollywood composer and the girl who is both his lyricist and love interest. (Hmm, I think I know these people.) And he wants *us* to do the music and lyrics. I finally have a private, major relationship in my life and discover it's about to be turned into a Broadway show. With music by Marvin Hamlisch, no less.

The script was about the emotional hardships that two songwriters run into when living and working together. There was some relief in that Neil often invented problems quite different from those Carole and I experienced. In fact, Neil never once sat me down and probed into what made me tick. My hopes, my fears, my Social Security number. Whatever parts of me he wrote into Vernon Gersh, the composer, one of the two leads, were things he perceived in my nature without having taken much time to find out. That was typical of Neil Simon: his instincts flying all over the place.

The meetings for *They're Playing Our Song* took place either at Neil's house or the one Carole and I were renting. We discussed the kind of song we needed in a scene; then Carole and I would go off and try to write something. Usually, Neil would make a suggestion, even come up with a title. I remember one meeting in particular. It was a Sunday afternoon, and Neil came over to our place for a light working brunch. Carole had her bean sprouts; Neil and I ordered out—bagels, smoked salmon, whitefish, pickles, cole slaw, potato salad, onion rings, and iced tea (with NutraSweet, of course). Nowadays, the working brunch consists of herbal tea and oat bran. That has two major advantages: One, the collaborators are always regular, and two, it gives you ten more years of life to yearn for a good corned beef sandwich.

Cholesterol aside, we were discussing the scene in which the two songwriters go out to a disco. It called for them to start dancing to one of the records on the jukebox. Well, I had trouble writing a song for them to sing in this scene, probably because I don't dance. Besides, Carole and I felt that if *we* were the characters in the scene, we'd hate dancing to someone else's music. By now, we weren't sure who was writing what for whom. (I mean, was it us or was it the characters?) Suddenly—I don't remember whose idea it was—we reached the conclusion that if the disco started playing one of Vernon and Sonia's songs (I mean, one of *our* songs), things might be different. They (we) would be thrilled to hear their (our) song being played.

One brainstorm rapidly led to another. Carole is talking animatedly, and Neil is exploding with ideas, and suddenly I am propelled out of my chair and running to the piano. (It had to be a good idea to get me away from the bagels and whitefish.) And I say: "If they started playing one of *my* songs, I'd probably say . . ." And now, making it up as I go along, I start playing and singing: "Ah ha they're playing *my* song, ah ha they're playing *my* song . . ." Neil is laughing hysterically, and Carole is writing her lyrics like a bat out of hell, and not only did we have a song, but we had a title for our show.

Things moved quickly. Neil, in addition to being a king of writers, is a king of rewriters, and he can tell in an instant what works and what doesn't. Over the next eight months, Carole and I had completed the score, and we went into rehearsal. The sweet smell of success came early. Tryouts in Los Angeles drew raves. Yes, there were some songs to change and here and there some fixing to do. But we were never in serious trouble.

As a matter of fact, Vernon and Sonia were doing much better than Marvin and Carole. *They're Playing Our Song* had a "happy ending." In the real world, when love and the professions mix, happy endings can be elusive. Competitiveness can be a serious obstacle. Since the age of seven, I had believed that success with music was the key ingredient to my happiness. I am praised; therefore, I am happy. (Descartes had it wrong.) When a lesson at Juilliard didn't go well, I was in trouble, brooding and sullen. If only I had been more like Vernon Gersh. He was confident. But *They're Playing Our Song*, though inspired by Carole's and my lives, was no real baring of my soul. Those who thought they were seeing the real Marvin Hamlisch up there on the stage were only watching a musical-comedy caricature.

They're Playing Our Song opened on Broadway to favorable reviews on February 11, 1979. I now had two shows running at the same time—*A Chorus Line*, at the Shubert, and *They're Playing Our Song*, across the street at the Imperial. There goes the neighborhood.

The show's music attracted adjectives like "lively," "exhilarating," "catchy," "hummable." To think, the first-night reviews of my music for *They're Playing Our Song* were much better than for *A Chorus Line*. At least on the morning after *Our Song* opened, I was able to walk down the street. This time there were no complaints from the cabbies: "That-a-way, Mr. Hamlisks. You wrote a beauty this time."

But then Hamlisch's Law struck again. *Click* . . . "This is too easy." Yes, something was bothering me. I knew from the word go that *They're Playing Our Song* was never meant to be the great, visionary American musical. It was basically an old-fashioned love story. It was meant to be pure entertainment. This was not a show to ponder and plumb for meaning.

I couldn't help thinking about *A Chorus Line*—a musical groundbreaker. I had learned a lot from Neil Simon, and it was comfortable writing with Carole. The score for *Our Song* was an easier, simpler one to write than the one for *A Chorus Line*. It was not a seamless score. There were nine songs in *They're Playing Our Song*, but I didn't feel the passion for them that I did for the ones in *A Chorus Line*. I came to realize that it was *this passion*, which goes to the depths of one's being, that needed to be the essential ingredient of the best of my work.

I saw a movie in which Glenn Close and James Woods are married and someone asks them the secret of a happy marriage. "Only one of us can go crazy at a time," says Glenn. That was the problem with Carole and me: we'd both go crazy simultaneously. When you share the same career as well as the same pillow, everything that happens to one of you affects the other. That's a shaky foundation on which to build a sturdy relationship. Perhaps it was my ego that got in the way. It just seemed that our lives together focused only on success. We spent hours talking incessantly about professional matters, and somehow I needed time to myself and to forget about the competitive world of show business. I found that impossible to do, and finally, Carole and I broke up.

Sometimes I would go to see *They're Playing Our Song* and wonder why its ending and "our" ending weren't the same. It wasn't to be. When you break up, you think of the things that caused the pain, but you also remember the good things that worked. It's those things, the *good* things, that you want back. But the realization that work alone would not bring happiness had a profound effect on me. I was despondent. I didn't have that many close friends to turn to, and I started to feel lonely again.

"Marvin, you've got two shows running on Broadway—what else do you want?" one of my friends said. I wanted them to realize that wasn't enough. For that was a life spent chasing the wrong rainbow. I started developing intense headaches. At first, I attributed them to sinus trouble. After the X rays of my sinuses turned up negative, I realized that the headaches had more to do with my mental than my physical state. Although it's hard to believe, considering all the Maalox I've consumed, most people who know me only from television think I'm the most contented, easygoing guy in the world. A real fun person to be with. They should only know. When people see me on a stage or on a late-night talk show, I'm projecting a certain persona. That person is me, all right, but it's the best of me. What people out there aren't seeing is the Marvin who, even with a hit like *A Chorus Line*, is never satisfied, the Marvin who punishes himself for failure or even success. As Woody Allen says in *Annie Hall*: "I have a very pessimistic view of life. . . . I feel that life is divided into the horrible and the miserable." I tend to think a lot. (My mother used to say, "Marvin, you have too much time to think.") While other people use this time in a worthwhile way, like taking time to read a good book, I take the time to think and ponder and worry. I dwell on everything that might go wrong. In the same way that I can recite only my bad reviews verbatim, I concentrate on the negative possibilities. It starts out with my wondering if I will ever be able to outdo *A Chorus Line*. I wonder if I will spend the rest of my life dissatisfied, endlessly striving, interminably alone. More and more I dig an ever-widening hole, one that soon gives rise to yet another blinding headache.

Can you imagine how Carole must have felt when she saw me despondent and pessimistic again and again? What I couldn't explain to her was that for me *They're Playing Our Song* wasn't enough. And I guess I could also see that this relationship wasn't enough, either. There was a kind of void; I still hadn't learned that important lesson—finding harmony between one's professional and personal life. I think I know today that one's personal life comes first. It's what makes the professional one worthwhile. Carole was gone now, and with no one else there, I went back to the only way I knew how to live—which was to work. This way, I could draw on the depths of my feelings for my music, but it still left me hiding behind an inner sense of terrible incompleteness.

10.

FREE-FALL

I desperately needed distractions, but keeping one's career at a certain level can be frustrating. Even with Broadway in my backyard, there were no magic words I could incant and have a musical materialize for me. So at the beginning of 1980, I accepted when Robert Redford asked me to adapt the music for his new film *Ordinary People*. In 1982, I did the score for *Sophie's Choice*, Alan Pakula's brilliant film. But except for flying out to California to do these scores, I was essentially in New York—and alone.

With the dreaded disease of time on my hands, I found myself at the piano several hours each day. I got back to writing songs again. But the fact of the matter was that the music business had changed radically since the days when Howard and I stalked the Brill Building. In the sixties, you could write songs for singers like Frank Sinatra, Tony Bennett, or Perry Como, with the hope that they would record them as singles and turn them into big hits. This was the way Jule Styne, Irving Berlin, Lieber and Stoller earned their keep. In those days, there were songwriters and there were singers. It was a kind of symbiosis. Then came the revolution: The Beatles, Carole King, Paul Simon, Elton John, Billy Joel. It was now the era of rock, rock bands, rock concerts, rock stars. And the thing about many rock stars was that they wrote their own songs. Very few of them turned to songwriters other than themselves. They wrote what they wanted, put what they wanted on their albums, and released them when they wanted to—in other words, they had total control. They never had to hear what I must've heard hundreds of times: "Stevie Wonder does his own music, Marvin" or "Diana is not wild about this, Marvin" or "We'll get back to you, Marvin." Rock stars don't have to wade through the morass of producers, A & R men, record-company executives, and the dozens of others up and down the ladder. I guess you got the message: This was not the best time for me to go back to songwriting. What was it the best time for?

In the summer of 1982, I felt something start to stir. A young man named Christopher Adler came to see me with an idea for a musical. Chris was the son of Richard Adler, who had cocreated the scores for *The Pajama Game* and *Damn Yankees*.

"Marvin," Chris said, "I'm not quite sure how to explain this to you."

"Try me."

"I have an idea. . . . It's for a musical. . . . I don't think you're really going to believe this."

I couldn't imagine why this was so difficult for him.

"It's sort of unbelievable, Marvin. Maybe I'll just leave you this ten-page treatment. Call me when you've had a chance to take a look."

He handed it to me. I didn't know what to make of his odd behavior. It wasn't until two days later that I looked at what he had left. I was totally confused at first. It *was* hard to believe. Yet the more I read, the more compelling the story became. It was shocking, heartbreaking, urgent, even dangerous. I was taken by the scope of it. But could this conceivably be made into a musical? It had to be one of the most audacious ideas ever envisioned for Broadway. But I could think of no more stunning test for my work at this point in my career.

It was also a political issue for me. The tale of this Iowa school-girl, if it ever succeeded, would resonate from New York to the corridors of power in Washington. This story woke me up, and now I wanted to disturb the sleep of the world. There were those who said it was crazy for me to have given up Hollywood to work on *A Chorus Line*. God knows what they would say now—that I was self-destructive or suicidal?—to want to make a musical of the life of this strange, haunted, politically radical heroine.

This young woman from Iowa received her first flash of fame when director Otto Preminger, after a vigorous nationwide search that rivaled the hunt for Scarlett O'Hara, found her in Marshalltown and chose her, a complete unknown, to play Joan of Arc in his movie *Saint Joan*. In a sense, the search had made this extraordinarily beautiful girl a star well before the film opened. Preminger had mounted one of the most elaborate publicity campaigns in the history of the cinema. The film was talked about for months, before it was ever seen in a movie house. Yet as is well known in the annals of movie history, *Saint Joan* was one of the worst of Preminger's several fiascos, overhyped, overdone, overadvertised, and awful. The young starlet received unanimously scathing reviews. She was panned in every newspaper and magazine across the country. Preminger was accused of having ruined this poor girl's career, and it was said in all the columns that she would "never work again." But in the very next two years she had proved herself a gifted, exhilarating actress, a truly international star, with two classics: *Bonjour Tristesse* and the incomparable *Breathless*. Neither Hollywood nor Otto Preminger could stop the beautiful Jean Seberg.

That's only half the story. The life of Jean Seberg was far more than the life of a movie actress. And this was what I responded to in Chris's treatment. This gifted international star was also a strangely political animal. In the sixties, she became seriously involved with the counterculture movement. She was an activist for civil rights, a radical, and became intensely involved with the Black Panthers. She clearly decided to throw her movie career to the winds. Ultimately, Seberg was targeted by the FBI and placed under constant surveillance. Her phone was tapped. There was pressure brought to bear not to let her work. She became a cause célèbre.

When she got pregnant, *Newsweek* ran an article insinuating that the baby she was carrying had been fathered by a black militant. This invasion of privacy troubled her so much that she miscarried late in her term. At the infant's funeral she insisted on opening the casket to prove that the baby was white. And it was this typical act of daring that exposed the lies of J. Edgar Hoover. It was due to Jean Seberg's bravery, and of others like her, that we owe the passage of the Freedom of Information Act.

But she had been victimized for too long. Her life became a nightmare of suspicion and paranoia. Everywhere she went she was watched. It became too much for her: at nearly forty-one, she committed suicide in the backseat of a car on a lonely Paris street, a statistic of the Establishment's revenge against radicalism.

Not since the idea of *A Chorus Line* had I felt I could extend the dimensions of my own music and still come to terms with the demands of commercial theatre. Yes, a story of a rebellious tragic heroine who kills herself could, I believed, be done in a

Broadway house. I didn't really care if anyone agreed with me. I thought a musical was a brilliant way to get the story of Jean Seberg finally out in the open. I called Chris Adler and let him know I was ready to go.

I wasn't surprised when friends told me I was nuts. But as I said to Christopher, I was overwhelmed by the Jean Seberg story. I saw her as a martyr, her fate as our country's tragedy. In Jean's story could be found the corruption that surrounds us everywhere and the prejudices that undermine our American dream. The whole thing had the pungent aroma of McCarthyism. I kept seeing Jean's courageous ability to bounce back again and again. I saw the panorama of the best of America (where an unknown can become a star) and the worst of America (where you can be destroyed by it). I hated the injustice of it all. My father had always believed in the greatness of this country—after all, he had been taken in as an exile from the Nazis—but now I started to wonder whether the America he had come to was as fair and open as he thought it was. Here was a chance to examine the truths we hold to be self-evident.

There was only one person who had the talent and imagination to grasp the dimensions I saw in this piece of our history. I took it to Michael Bennett. He saw it instantly: He agreed that this could make a truly American masterpiece. With Michael to second the motion, I threw all caution to the winds. We began to work. Chris Adler had mentioned a librettist to me, Julian Barry, who he thought would be perfect. Julian had written a play about Lenny Bruce, and you couldn't get any more political than that. Michael and Julian set out to develop a script, while Christopher and I began to hammer out lyrics and music. The first songs we did reflected the midwestern idealism of Iowa prairie country; others were stronger, brooding, almost operatic in nature. We were finding our way; we were capturing this political drama in musical terms. Michael heard what we had done. He was overwhelmed. We had fed his theatrical instincts, fired his imagination, and he was filled with ideas.

"Marvin," he told me, "you've opened my eyes to something here. I'm with you all the way on this. I think we can leave a mark with this one." Michael took me aside and looked at me with those burning eyes: "Thanks, Marvin."

I could barely contain myself. Michael had at least ten possible projects on his plate. When I came to him with *Jean*, I wasn't sure he'd feel about it the way I did or whether he'd be willing to put everything aside to work with me on this. And now with Michael on board, my vision of *Jean* grew and grew and became almost limitless. I was reminded of the old *Chorus Line* workshop days. Chris and I worked constantly, while Michael and Julian were hammering out a script. I was exhausted, but I never gave it a second thought.

We had to make sure the music was varied enough; we invented comic moments as relief from the drama; Michael used his sense of the theatrical to the maximum—almost to the point of tour de force. More than anything, we had to find a way of making Jean's suicide inspire the audience—to make them see what she did as heroic. We didn't want it to come off as heavy or harsh or morbid. In about six weeks, we had gone a long way toward molding a first act.

Michael was driven; I hadn't ever seen him so stimulated. We used to talk on the phone at night for hours. There were times I could barely believe this was happening and that Michael and I were working together again. It didn't get much better than that.

And then a strange, unaccountable darkness fell over all of it.

One night, there was a message from my lawyer to call him immediately. It was urgent. When we talked, he told me that something peculiar was going on. He asked me if Michael had said anything to me lately that sounded odd. I told him, "No. In fact, the work is moving along feverishly."

"Marvin, something's going on. Michael seems to have rocks in his head."

"What do you mean?" I asked him.

"I mean that every offer we've made comes back with a 'no.' You tell me this guy's dying to do this show and we offer him six percent and his lawyer comes back and says he wants eight. I'm willing to bet that if I offer him eight, he'll want ten. This Michael Bennett is a piranha."

"I can't believe what you're telling me."

"Marvin, I think the handwriting's on the wall: He wants out."

But I knew that Michael didn't want out. I knew he hadn't lost his enthusiasm. If anything, he was more excited about Jean Seberg and the politics of America than he had ever been. I also knew that Michael wasn't shy about telling me what he thought. If there was an artistic problem, Michael wouldn't hide it from me. He was famous for telling you what was on his mind—no matter how much he knew it would hurt.

No, I was too close to Michael. The demand for money had to be a cover-up for something else. It finally dawned on me that at the heart of this must have been some sort of fallout from the political sensitivity of the Jean Seberg story. I might have been getting a bit paranoid, but I don't think so. Was this life story too dangerous for the makers and shakers of Broadway? I became infuriated, frustrated, angry. Could someone have actually scared Michael off? In my wildest dreams I could never let myself believe that. I decided to confront him.

"Michael, what the hell is going on? You've been behind *Jean* from the moment I brought it to you. You, more than anyone else, understood my vision here—the theatrical implications, the musical implications, and, above all, the political implications. And now my lawyer tells me that you won't make a deal. After we've gone this far? After what we've been through together? Michael, Jean Seberg's story has to be told."

For the first time since I had known him, he was unable to answer me. He seemed sullen and quiet. And then all he could bring himself to say was "I'm sorry. I can't do it."

What was I to do without Michael? I was totally bewildered. This was as let down as I'd ever been. I thought about calling it quits but realized I wouldn't let Jean down. I was ready to go out on a limb and risk all. But it became like a crusade—to prove to Michael that I could go it alone and that I could make it work. I started to search frantically for a new director. Several turned us down flat, and I remember one of them saying: "I wouldn't touch the Jean Seberg story no matter what. It's too hot to handle."

I must admit that one or two directors were willing to take on the show, but I thought they were wrong for the project. I had recently seen *Amadeus* in London. It was brilliant, brash, and inventive. It was directed by Peter Hall, who has had a long, distinguished career in the theatre, and I wondered to myself if he might possibly be right for *Jean*. I invited him to New York to hear the score. He was dazzled by it and, even more, was terribly intrigued by the story. I had no doubt that he had empathy for Jean and that he was politically in tune with what had happened to America in the sixties. My only shadow of a doubt was whether he fully understood how to do this as a musical.

There was another reservation. Peter Hall insisted, if he was to direct, that the show first be mounted in London at his National Theatre. I had never thought of *Jean* being anything other than an American musical. But I was won over by Peter's enthusiasm. Opening in jolly old England was a chance worth taking. But this may have been the single greatest professional mistake of my life. To transplant a show five thousand miles to another culture was a tremendous lack of insight on my part. In its very marrow, the story was an American phenomenon.

Rehearsals began in London on September 5, 1983. And now we come to one of the great ironies, one that demonstrates how blissfully ignorant I was in the ways of the British theatre. To my horror, from day one, I watched the British press indict Peter Hall and the "ugly Americans" for exploiting the National Theatre, using it for what they constantly referred to as "an out-of-town tryout." What they obviously resented was that the National Theatre had been intended as a repertory theatre, and even though Peter Hall was its director, they clobbered him for bringing something American to their English showplace.

Clearly, this was not the ideal atmosphere to fuel the creative spirit. From my point of view, the issue was getting the Jean Seberg story produced, not taking advantage of a national institution. That was the farthest thing from my mind. Yet the next thing I knew, the British press had labeled me the composer who had bamboozled the British. I felt as if the second Battle of Britain had begun. The atmosphere got worse, not better. *Jean* had undergone a sea change, all right, and the mighty Atlantic was never calm again. We worked on despite the odds. We had script troubles, but they were working themselves out. The score was nearly finished. And then, one afternoon, Peter came to rehearsal and told us he'd been thinking of a new idea: "I'd like to try something. It strikes me that we might solve a major problem by not having just one Jean but by having two. I mean the young Jean and the older Jean, both onstage at the same time. I want the older Jean to look back at her life, as if this were some kind of memory play."

This sounded like it might work theatrically, though I

doubted it. I watched the next week of rehearsals. We now had two Jeans. But instead of clarifying the show, it tore it apart. I was convinced that Peter had made a crucial error. This certainly wasn't the show we had written. We had conceived of a tour de force for a major star. The score was a bravura one for the lead character, and by evening's end, one hoped the audience really understood her resilience as she poured her heart into song after song, scene after scene. We wanted to start with the young Jean and play her through to her suicide. It struck me that Peter's device dissipated the drama and the score. In short, two Jeans made the whole thing confusing. Slowly, but oh, so surely, I saw *Jean* slipping out of my grasp. For one thing, this "double" concept was a notion that came too late in the game. Had we agreed from the outset that there would be a young Jean and an older one, it might have been possible to make it work. But that was never the premise. The attempt to revamp a show so drastically just before its opening was too difficult a task to undertake at the eleventh hour. For the audience to empathize with Jean's courage and tenacity, the focus must be on one person, not two. Once she became two, I felt it was like taking *Gypsy* and dividing Rose into twins. As the previews began, there was no doubt that we were in deep trouble. And no amount of fixes would help.

There are really only two ways to destroy a show. One is by overworking a bad idea. Whatever you do to it, you can't change the underlying weakness. The other is to take a good idea and do it badly. That's what happened with *Jean*. The strengths of the show were lost in a misconceived production. The British press was unanimous. The show was a flop, which ended its chance of ever coming to Broadway. I'll take the rap for that. Once the music had to be revised for two Jeans, I lost my stride. It hurt reading the reviews, particularly because I agreed with them. Yet I continue to believe that there's something scary and sinister about Jean's story, that there's still a desperate need to show what happened—and can still happen—when the American dream goes wrong. Maybe you have to be an American and have lived through McCarthyism to understand the emotional impact of the Jean Seberg story.

It wasn't until I was back in New York that it sank in that the Marvin Hamlisch who had won all the awards had a full-fledged disaster. Being vulnerable was not part of the master plan. I stayed in my apartment a lot. I was obsessed with the failure of *Jean*. I went over and over it in my mind. I thought of the early days, when we had all begun—Chris Adler, Julian Barry, myself, and, of course, Michael. I thought over and over about what might have been. I kept hearing Michael's voice on the day he told me: "I'm sorry. I can't do it."

The story of Jean *doesn't really end here, and although I've never told this story before, I'm compelled to tell it now. Years after I had come back from England, I discovered that Michael Bennett was ill and fighting a losing battle with AIDS. I flew out west to see him in the hospital. He was ghostly and weak, but he wanted to talk. His eyes lit up when we reminisced about* A Chorus Line *and how much it had changed our lives. We talked about some of the kids in the show and how they were doing.*

A nurse came in. It was time to leave now. And just as I bent over to say my good-byes, Michael said he had something to tell me.

"Marvin, I always wanted to do Jean. *Always. It was never the money. But I can tell you now there was political pressure on me—it was enormous—not to touch the Jean Seberg story. They made me bow out. I shouldn't have."*

* * *

Having hit rock bottom with *Jean*, I wasn't sure where I was headed. I wasn't ready to go back to Broadway (not that the phone was ringing off the hook). I still needed time to lick the wounds. I had to wait it out, which is the way it sometimes goes in show business. But yours truly and waiting are natural enemies. No, I thought to myself, Marvin has to make music.

There had always been, and still were, dozens of invitations to guest conduct with major orchestras across the country. The idea was to do my own "pops" evening, conducting my own music and film scores and having the thrill of hearing it played by some of the finest musicians in America. The repertoire would be built around *The Way We Were*, *The Sting*, and *A Chorus Line*. There would also be some Gershwin and Leonard Bernstein.

I made my debut with the Minnesota Orchestra. Then followed evenings with the Pittsburgh Symphony, the Dallas Symphony, and the beloved Boston Pops. Hearing what I had written reverberating from concert halls coast to coast was the perfect bromide for my bomb across the sea. Speaking of which, something unexpected happened. I was asked to be the guest artist with the venerable London Symphony Orchestra. (The last time I heard anyone mention the word "London," I was at Heathrow Airport being booted out of town with a stash of unfavorable reviews under my arm.) But never one to leave terrible enough alone, I boarded British Air, praying the pilot had not seen *Jean*. To my delight, the concert was a huge success, the London Symphony Orchestra played Hamlisch magnificently, the reception was splendid, and even the press forgave, and forgot.

After London, it was back on the road in America. I continued going from one major orchestra to another, conducting and playing my music. Another big bonus of my concert career (in addition to the checks) was that for the first time this native West Side New Yorker was seeing America. I knew every major mall there was to know. People who work in Hollywood and on Broadway lead a bicoastal life; they see the East Coast and L.A., the Plaza and the Polo Lounge. The rest are what one network executive called "the people we fly over." I started to see a lot of them, and they left me with stories I love to tell.

I once gave a concert with the Atlanta Symphony Orchestra. During the show I jokingly remarked: "I love to eat. But I must confess I have a problem down here. So far, all the restaurants I've dined at in Atlanta have the most delicious ribs. Unfortunately, they all are *pork* ribs. Now, I happen to be of the Jewish persuasion." (I wasn't exactly persuaded. I was *told*.) "I don't eat pork ribs, so I really wish I could lay my hands on some barbecued beef ribs."

Well, that evening, as I was walking back to my hotel from the symphony hall, this woman approaches me.

"Mahvin, honey," she says in a rich southern drawl, "Ah want you to come on over to mah house tomorrow night. We're gonna give you a real Georgia party."

That sounded fine to me. Next evening, after the concert, a white Rolls-Royce pulled up to the stage door, and a liveried chauffeur came to my dressing room and escorted me to the car. We then drove for miles into the countryside. These were the rolling hills where the young Margaret Mitchell was first inspired to write *Gone With the Wind*. At each mansion we passed I expected to see the O'Haras arriving for a cookout with the Wilkeses. We finally arrived at a house where in a single day my host had assembled 150 guests. The swimming pool and the trees were flooded by pin lights, and a great party was in progress.

As I walked under the portico, she said: "Mahvin honey, before yah meet anyone, Ah want you to sit yourself down a minute."

And she showed me to a table where she had set up a service for one. It shone with sparkling crystal and gleaming silver. There in the middle, on the largest dinner plate this side of the Mason-Dixon line, was a huge bowl of *beef* ribs. And that's how one New Yorker was introduced to southern hospitality.

There was the time I was giving a performance for General Motors' top executives at the Waldorf-Astoria. Roger Smith, the president of GM, was present as I recounted the story of this rich lady with the southern drawl who treated me so regally in Georgia.

I turned to Roger Smith and said: "I know that you must be a rather generous man, and I'm sure you wouldn't want to be outdone by my good friend from Georgia. So let me say that I've always been a great admirer of Cadillacs. I really like royal blue. Convertible." I waited to see if he would match the generous spirit of the South. And that evening, believe it or not, I think I touched Roger Smith's heart. He sent me a car, all right. It was a tiny replica that you pin on your lapel.

One of the places I most wanted to play was Wolf Trap, the famous outdoor theatre near Washington, D.C. I finally got my wish. I had a contract to play there with the Fairfax Symphony Orchestra. So I flew to Washington, came to the theatre, and found the orchestra rehearsing their part of the program. They would provide the first half of the evening, and I would appear with them after the intermission. I decided that while the orchestra was still working on its own program, it would be a good time for me to eat. (When isn't it a good time to eat?)

So I went to lunch. When I returned to the theatre, I made a disturbing discovery. The orchestra was gone. Gone.

They must be on a fifteen-minute break, I thought. But after half an hour, I approached the stage manager.

"Where's the orchestra?" I said.

"They've gone home," she said.

"When are they coming back to rehearse with me?"

"They're not."

It seems that someone had failed to tell the orchestra that I was to perform with them. Just a little administrative error and seventy-five musicians had scattered to all parts of Maryland, Virginia, and the District of Columbia. It was now three o'clock in the afternoon of the day of the concert, and I am going—I believe the precise psychological term is "bananas." I called my agent in New York and screamed: "These people in Washington are crazy!"

"You should have seen the Carter administration," he replied.

I was frantic. I didn't know what to do. And then it struck me that one of the beauties of the piano is that you don't need an orchestra. Think of Horowitz. Think of Chico Marx. Think of Richard Nixon. All right, don't think of Richard Nixon.

During the first half, as scheduled, the Fairfax Symphony performed. Then, as if I had the plague, all the musicians scampered from their chairs, leaving an empty stage and a lonely piano. And a lonely Marvin Hamlisch gave a solo performance that lasted over an hour.

I was amused to see in one of the Washington papers the next morning a perceptive music critic who wrote something like this:

Mr. Hamlisch and the symphony orchestra were both in fine form. One would hope that some day soon they might be able to perform together.

* * *

One thing that Liza didn't tell me about going on the road was that if you're single, there are more benefits than just applause. I found that for a bachelor the Midwest exercised a special charm. After most of my concerts, there was a reception at which I would meet some of the sweetest, prettiest girls you can imagine. (And I have a vivid imagination.) They were on the planning committee or in the group sponsoring the concert. And there I was, gleaming in my tuxedo, in the middle of all these single lovelies. They kept stressing the fact that they just adored "The Way We Were" and how passionate they felt about the heartbreaking lyrics. Naturally I refrained from telling them that I only wrote the music. Here I was, just a pale, bespectacled composer whose hands were fondling nothing but a keyboard. I once said to my drummer: "It's a shame that we come in and out of these towns so fast, because I guarantee that I could easily fall in love right here on the spot."

Yes, I had fallen in love with much of America. I must have done fifty concerts, twenty-four barbecues, and sixteen lectures at local music schools—you name it. I started to feel as if I were running for office. But during one of the last concerts of the season, I started longing to compose again. *Click* . . . "All your years at Juilliard may have made conducting seem very vital and laudable, but where's *your* music?" There was still a part of me that felt unfulfilled. For one thing, I couldn't shake the persistent, pesky inner voice of the composer part of me. For another, I had just had an offer to do a Broadway musical based on the film *Smile*.

The movie had been written by Jerry Belson and directed by Michael Ritchie, and it dealt with the shenanigans of the finalists in the "Young American Miss" competition. I liked the idea.

I was more determined than ever to write about our American values, and what better subject than beauty pageants. Now we all know that these pageants are supposed to honor the "best" values in American life. Yet they are often venomous little events that bring friendly competition to the heights of hysteria. It was fertile ground to write songs against such an ironic backdrop. I wanted to capture the fabulous tongue-in-cheek quality that had made the movie a cult classic.

The basic issue, right from the start, was to decide whether to grin or sneer. The show had to be a spoof of these pageants and yet needed to be satirical and tough. I had been told of a talented guy named Howard Ashman, who had created the hit musical *Little Shop of Horrors*. (Years later, Howard would receive Oscars for his brilliant work on *The Little Mermaid* and *Beauty and the Beast*.) I met him and liked him very much but was wary when he demanded that he not only write the book and lyrics but direct the show as well. The trouble with wearing three hats is that it can crush you like an avalanche. And for this very reason, working with Howard proved very difficult: On Monday, it was a shouting match with Howard the Book Writer; on Tuesday, it was a confrontation with Howard the Director; and on Wednesday, it was trying to write a song with Howard the Lyricist. The dynamics were all wrong, but it taught me a hard lesson, and I've sworn it will never happen to me again. I knew this collaboration wasn't going to work, but the pull of the theatre had gripped me, as it always will.

The trouble was with the focus of the show; Howard kept moving between satire and celebration. The truth is, we were trying to have it both ways: a witty indictment of the values promoted by beauty pageants and, at the same time, a real live extravaganza of what we were supposed to be ridiculing. The point of view of a show is absolutely critical; it can't change or vacillate. On the one hand, we were not bold enough to do a "dark comedy." On the other hand, what we didn't want was a beauty pageant of a musical. What was up on the stage was a hybrid; not this, not that. We were clearly floundering. And if we couldn't make up our minds, how could the audience?

We had problems in rehearsals. They were nothing to compare to what faced us out of town in Baltimore. I was actually living what I had once witnessed during the out-of-town tryouts of *Funny Girl*. I was writing new songs at night, rehearsing them for eight hours the next day, then back to the drawing board in the evening—day in and day out. I was in the thick of it. It was a far cry from the days of being a rehearsal pianist for Buster Davis. Then, there wasn't much for me to lose. The show was changing like mad, but it wasn't getting better. Nor was the music. I was frazzled and exhausted. It was time to summon help, and I knew it.

Tommy Tune flew to Baltimore. He was quick to see what was wrong, and he was brutally honest. He didn't think much of the show. And as I already suspected, he was right. The book was awkward, the score was corny, although I had meant it to be satirical, and the production numbers were feeble at best.

Lyndon Johnson used to tell a story about a boy who applies for a job on a railroad line that is being built near his Texas home. The foreman asks him a question: "What would you do if you were standing by the switch and you saw two locomotives converging on one another on the same track?" The boy says he would get his brother. "Why on earth would you get your brother?" asks the foreman. "Because he's never *seen* a train wreck."

Well, I was about to see one helluva train wreck, and there was nothing to smile about. The show opened in New York on November 24, 1986. The headlines speak for themselves: the *New York Post*: "Guarded Smile." *Newsday*: "An Empty Smile."

USA Today: "Sunshiny but Shallow Smile." And the *Daily News* personalized it with "Marvin Misses." You can't buy that kind of publicity.

Friends would say, "Forget it, don't worry. For God's sake, let's see you smile." Just hearing that word put me on antidepressants for weeks. I could envision what life had in store for me: My elevator man would start letting me off on the wrong floor. I dreaded the day the building co-op board would meet. I could hear them saying: "That Hazlick has got to go." Even worse, when I'd rush for a cab, just as I got close, the off-duty sign would go on. Then the cabbie would roll down his window and shout: "Hey, Marvin. I spent forty bucks for my wife to see that *Smile* show you wrote. It ain't no *Chorus Line*."

Yes, I knew it wasn't *A Chorus Line*. I'd seen it as a hilarious spoof, quirky and wholesome; there was also to be an element of social satire. But I couldn't deliver. It never jelled. I pondered the future and spent a lot of time in my apartment. It was needed time, because it gave me a chance to reflect about the past and the work I'd done.

And lately, that work wasn't very good at all. I couldn't help but think: 1974, the Oscars; 1975, *A Chorus Line*; but then, in 1983, *Jean*; in 1986, *Smile*. Something had gone terribly wrong. Not since *They're Playing Our Song* had I had a bona fide hit. What followed were three very tough years for me, years without any writing offers of much consequence. It's funny, celebrity status. Even without having a current hit, I was still invited to all the parties, all the opening nights. And when someone asked me: "What are you doing, Marvin?" I'd smile sheepishly and say: "I'm working on a new project."

But there wasn't one. They kept asking the question. And I kept lying.

By the end of 1987, I became very depressed. Part of me knew that other projects would come in their own time and in their own way, but being idle and alone was still agony. I also had to put to rest the child in me that still saw things in black and white, success or failure. I struggled to understand that there are a lot of shades in between, that success or failure is only one of life's several yardsticks.

Dashiell Hammett once told Lillian Hellman: "It's only fame, Lilly. It's just a paint job. It doesn't have anything to do with writing." Why didn't I know that early on? Somehow, after *Jean* and *Smile*, I should have brushed myself off and started all over again. If only I could have gone back to writing music. But all I could do was eat myself up alive. And my thoughts haunted me. Every day I woke up thinking: Were my early successes with *A Chorus Line* and *The Way We Were* going to be my last ones? Were those "the good old days"? My confidence slowly drained away, my doubts grew and grew, and the go-getter, work-work-and-more-work man I'd been up till now became horribly withdrawn.

A gray cloud came over me, and there didn't seem to be any sun in the forecast. Up to now, I never worried about where my next assignment would come from, what I would write, or my aim in writing it. But for a period of over three years, I wasn't able to write much, and Hollywood and Broadway certainly weren't banging down my door.

I felt myself in free-fall, falling into a life of nonexistence. What was there to look forward to? Would I ever achieve something again? Had I blown it by doing it all when I was so young? I was in despair. Did I have anything more to give?

For so long, I had looked at success with myopic vision. I had put all my eggs in that "success basket." But careers have a way of righting themselves, and deep down, I had to grapple with the realization that my headaches and my depression were caused by more than just career setbacks.

My state of mind was masking the real source of trouble and no amount of antidepressants would work. I needed to come face-to-face with what was at the root of all this. I guess I'd been on a treadmill since I was six, and it had started at Juilliard. I guess I never got off. I had, in many ways, lived up to my master plan, but I realized now that there was always something missing in my strategy. I had never set aside enough thought or time or, sadly, enough emotion to seek out someone to be with, someone who cared about me—and someone I cared about.

It was dawning on me that without this in my life there was no amount of success that would really fulfill my needs. Even had *Jean* and *Smile* been megahits, I would still be walking home alone, making my way to my apartment, greeting the doorman, taking the elevator, opening the door of my apartment, finding it comfortable and clean—with the piano perfectly in place—but empty.

I looked around the living room. If this was where all these years had led me, I knew I had a great deal of changing to do.

11.

TELEPHONE TERRE

One of the problems in show business is that you meet a lot of show-bizzy people. Now, don't get me wrong. I love show business, but I'm pretty old-fashioned. The fast lane was never for me. Billy Wilder once said, "I was married once, now I just lease." Not for me. I liked the family atmosphere in which I was raised. I didn't have to be at every "A" party. I'm the kind of guy who occasionally used to put in an appearance, get turned off by the smell of marijuana, and then head for home. I wasn't attracted by what often passed for marriage in Hollywood. The brides there kept the bouquets and threw away the grooms. My aim was a time-honored, traditional married life. Something out of an Irving Berlin ballad.

Of course, by now you know that I never allowed myself the time it took for a real relationship. The people I knew best were the cabdrivers who took me to Queens College and the guys who delivered the Moviolas to my apartment. Occasionally, I did have a date, but with my hectic schedule, I never seemed to follow up. Even when the sparks of a relationship began to flicker, they somehow fizzled out. I had a few near Mrs., but somehow things always turned sour. The first really important romance I had when I was very young was with a girl at college. She was in a program where they exchanged students, and she went to Paris. When she returned, she had taken on the French quality to which any tourist can testify. She hated Americans. She felt that Americans were the worst. We no longer had anything to talk about. Everything in America was horrible. It was all so "bourgeois." At first, I tried to kid it away. "I'll have a bourgeois Coke," I'd say. "Maybe a bourgeois hamburger. No, I think I'll have some bourgeois french fries. Very French." If someone asked, "What car are you driving?" I'd reply, "I drive a Bourgeois." No matter what, things never turned out right.

There was the gorgeous coed who always loved it when I played her a song. Unfortunately for me, however, I didn't have a piano in the bedroom, so the relationship never blossomed. Or the one who was crazy for me, told me she didn't care about my music, only me, me, me. Oh, yes, and jewelry. And then a few years later there was Karen. I liked Karen, but she had no ear for music. We used to play a little game. She'd sing one of my songs, and I'd try to guess what it was. And then after that there was Tovah. She liked to read detective stories in Yiddish and tell me who the killer was. There was Wanda. She was into culture. She'd take me to little art houses to see Chinese movies without subtitles. In my early thirties there was Charlotte. I had great hopes for her. I played her a song I'd just written, and she said, "You just wrote that?" And I said, "Oh, it's nothing." And she said, "Yes, that's what I thought." Then there was Georgette, who was very nice, but she seemed a little bit aloof. So in a moment of frankness I said: "Georgette, sometimes you seem a little pretentious." And she said: "*Moi?*"

Of course, many of my dates were from show business. That's how Carole Bayer Sager and I met and became so attached to each other. But it was hard for me to meet women who were outside of show business. I've never been in a singles bar. I don't know how to light up a cigarette, sidle up to a woman, and say: "Can I buy you a drink?" No, that's just not my style, though I realize it worked wonders for Robert Mitchum.

There were women who liked me a lot but couldn't stand my erratic ways, particularly when it came to my schedule. This proved fatal when I was on tour with symphony orchestras. I'd say I'd meet them next weekend, then something would come up, and I'd have to cancel. That habit, plus those still wretched, untimely headaches, and I'd lose another prospect. Unlike some celebrities in the entertainment world, I didn't get a lot of expressions of affection in fan letters. I didn't get proposals of marriage or suggestions for other interesting arrangements. What's wrong with you people out there? I wondered. The closest I came to an anonymous expression of ardor was when I once opened an issue of *Playboy* magazine and found that the centerfold lady had chosen as "Favorite Musician: Marvin Hamlisch." I collapsed. I thought: This is impossible. A girl who's taking off her clothes for the world to see and she likes me! If she liked me so much, she could've called, right?

But whatever the reasons, I was reaching forty-five, and I had not found the right woman for me. My dear friend, Richard Kagan, tried to fix me up. We had met when we were music counselors at an all-girls' camp. To this day, I still think that was the best job I ever had. It was there that I learned certain helpful phrases that seemed to work wonders with eighteen-year-olds. The one that worked for me was "I *need* you. Don't you understand, I *really need* you." (If you emphasize the word "really," trust me, it'll work wonders.) Richard and I remained friends over the years, and he started his own life insurance company in Los Angeles. He always kept an eye on me, like a brother.

And he watched me attempt one so-called relationship after another. Following one of my breakups in 1984, I went out to California to visit with him and his family for rest, consolation, and filial friendship. By now, Richard was well versed in the fortunes of my life with women. He developed a stock admonition: "Marvin," he said, "I know this breakup is tough on you, but it's like falling off a horse. You have to climb right back up there. And whether you know it or not, you're happier than you think when you're not alone."

"But Richard," I told him, "every time it doesn't work out, I am crushed. I don't think I want to go through this anymore."

For better or for worse, I decided I had had it with dating. I was ready to sell the memoirs of my love life to Nintendo and let them make a video game out of it. For five years I went pretty much cold turkey. But old reliable Richard had other ideas for me. Every time I visited him, he would persist in his matchmaking.

So it was with trepidation that toward the end of 1988, I listened to him one day, during a phone call from L.A. to New York.

"Marvin," Richard began, "you know our housekeeper, Maria?"

I certainly did. During my many visits to the Kagans, I had noticed that Maria was very nice and hardworking, a real find.

"Well, Maria has a sister, Rosa, who is also a housekeeper. Rosa was over the other day, and she told Maria about this fantastic woman that she works for. Her name is Terre Blair. Rosa says she is very beautiful, kind, really something special, but that she never goes out."

"Why not?"

"She just doesn't like the people she's been meeting, I guess."

"Richard, give me a break," I pleaded. "I am off the dating

circuit. You can alert the media. I love you, pal, but you are driving me crazy. I appreciate what you are trying to do, but I have enough aggravation."

"Marvin," he persisted, "Maria wouldn't steer you wrong." Well, the Kagan house was always so spotless that I couldn't help but agree with him.

"But on one condition," I said. "This will be the last time you do this. Will you promise?"

"I promise."

The scrap of paper that I scrawled Terre's number on stayed near the phone in the living room for close to a week. Thankfully, it never fell to the floor or behind the table or was swept up by *my* fantastic housekeeper, Shirley. I guess housekeepers have some unwritten code when it comes to matchmaking for their employers.

Richard, naturally, kept nagging. So finally, in my rather no frills and direct manner, I made the phone call—only to reach an answering machine. When it finished with what it had to say, I said: "Hi, this is Marvin Hamlisch. This is my number. Please call back." Bang. As far as I was concerned, I had kept my part of the bargain.

But neither Richard nor Rosa had remembered to tell Terre to expect my call. So when she got this message, she decided not to answer it. She must have thought it was some practical joke. Or, if she thought it was the real Marvin Hamlisch, she might have figured that I was some phony right out of the music business, into drugs and liquor. (Musicians have great reputations, don't they?) While she was talking on the phone to her friend Linda Willows, Terre told her about the bizarre phone message from some guy passing himself off as Marvin Hamlisch.

"Why would he be calling me and who gave him my number?" Terre asked.

"Who cares? Maybe it was him. I think you should call back. Maybe he'll ask you out. I mean, you're always stuck in your apartment."

"C'mon, Linda. I don't want to go out with some show-business type. I hate all that."

"Terre, he's a wonderful composer. Those melodies sound like they must come from his heart. I don't think he's going to be that bad. Besides, you don't have to marry him."

"Linda, there's no reason—"

Linda interrupted her again.

"Terre, if you don't at least call him back, I'm never going to speak to you." With that, she hung up the phone. Here was Terre's friend of four years telling her that their friendship would be null and void because of one unreturned phone call. Terre thought about this. She went to the phone. She picked it up. She made the call, but not quite. First she called Linda back. But Linda wouldn't answer the phone. Terre called again. Still no answer. Finally, in desperation and to preserve a friendship, Terre dialed my number.

She got *my* machine. Given the mood she was in, she left a message that rivaled mine in charm and length. "Hi. This is Terre Blair. Please call back." Bang. So far, isn't this romantic? For the next seven days we played telephone tag. And then, finally, we connected. I couldn't help but be struck by how down-to-earth she sounded. Though the conversation was short, I knew that I'd be calling back. I was careful to take her number from that scrap of paper and transfer it, in ink, to my address book. Within a few days, I had memorized it, anyway.

We talked about everything. Whatever came to our minds was fair game: music, life, spirituality, the differences in our religion, me, her, old-fashioned ideas, houses, L.A., Ohio (she was from Columbus). And after every call, I found my spirits rising three steps at a time. Terre was a graduate of Otterbein College near Columbus, Ohio. A small-town girl, she became a star on local television. She had been tremendously successful before the cameras and was catapulted to ABC's *Wide World of Sports* as well as New York's *Evening Magazine*. But the thing about Terre was that she quickly became disenchanted with all the hype and the politics behind the scenes, and at this point she wasn't sure if she wanted to continue with a television career—she had little patience with the phoniness that was all around her. So here were two people, both in show business but both very non–show business in nature. And on the phone we talked about everything except our careers. I'd often wonder whether if anyone heard our conversations, they'd ever guess we both had careers at all. I became addicted to phone calls to Terre.

After several weeks went by, I decided to send her something. But I didn't know what. I guess you're supposed to send flowers. I wanted her to know how much she was starting to mean to me, and so I called a florist in L.A. and told him to put together a mini–botanical garden. We are talking greenhouse here. Maybe I should have sent trees. But I worried that her landlord would raise the roof. He'd have to. When the flowers arrived, Terre called to tell me that her apartment couldn't hold them all, but she sounded like a little girl on her birthday. It was her constantly buoyant nature, her perennial optimism that I was falling for. The phone conversations got longer and longer; they were now averaging two hours a call.

During the second month of this long-distance marathon, I happened to mention one of the drawbacks of Los Angeles. My favorite ice cream flavor, Ben & Jerry's Heath Bar Crunch, was easy to get in New York but tough to get when I was on the Coast. I told her that for me this was an appalling, anxiety-provoking situation. From Terre, a non–ice cream devotee, this did not rouse much sympathy. But wouldn't you know, two days later, there was a knock at my apartment door.

"Hey, is this where the party is?"

"What party?" I asked.

"Well, I've got an order for twelve gallons of Ben and Jerry's here." The delivery man unloaded it in the kitchen. Terre never failed to amaze me. She had called the main plant and arranged the whole thing. Just when I was wondering where I was going to put all of this stuff, there was another knock on the door.

"Who's there?" I asked.

"It's me again. I've got twelve gallons more."

The calls kept getting longer. One of them lasted seven hours. (Thankfully, I called her collect.) We talked from 11:00 P.M. right through till 6:00 A.M., when I had to leave to catch a plane for Washington. By now we had been doing our telephone talkathon for over three months, and my instincts told me this odd, strange, bizarre, unheard-of relationship was right. I had never even seen this woman, yet I had made up my mind. I told my housekeeper, Shirley: "Okay, that's it. Clear out the closets." The chief beneficiary of this cleaning-out campaign was my cousin Melvyn in Chicago. He, too, is a forty-two long.

By now I suppose you're wondering how long this phantom romance could go on. I suppose you're even wondering if Marvin Hamlisch could get married without ever having seen his bride. No, emphatically not. During one of our phone calls, Terre told me she was coming to the Midwest at the beginning of February to do a television taping. This was it.

"I have an idea," I told her. "If you're already halfway across the country, why don't you come all the way to New York? Then we can finally meet."

Was this to be the beginning or the end, I wondered. We picked a specific date, February 6, 1989. Like Judy Garland and Robert Walker under the clock. But I told Terre: "If you get a better offer, say, Springsteen calls, let's face it, he's got the big bucks, I'd say yes."

The next day, Terre sent me a note: "Bruce Springsteen asked me out for February sixth, but I told him I had a previous engagement." With the note were just three roses. "Here's to you, me, and us." I liked the roses, but I loved the billing.

Terre was coming into New York on the evening of the fifth, staying at the Westbury Hotel, but we would wait until 11:00 A.M. on the morning of the sixth to actually meet. I waited for her phone call to tell me she had arrived. I was a man with both feet firmly planted in the clouds. That evening, she called. She started off very matter-of-factly, and I thought everything was great. It wasn't.

"Marvin," she said, her voice much more tentative than I had ever heard it before, "Marvin, this is all crazy. Forget it. It's been wonderful on the phone, but I mean—" There was so much that had gone so well on the phone, she felt there was too much to lose. She had another misgiving, too. She was still worried that I was in show business, which did not enchant her. She wasn't going to unpack. She was on her way back to Los Angeles.

I pleaded with her to stay. "Look, I'm really a family man. I'm not at all into the show-business scene. I have a snapshot of my house on Long Island. It's got a playground in the back, for God's sake. It doesn't even have a wet bar. I'll bring it over."

"No, you can't come over tonight," said Terre.

"I can send it by messenger."

"I don't think so."

"I'm really into home and stuff like that," I said. I was pleading like a convict before the parole board. I tried everything. Finally, she agreed to stay the next day. And if for some reason it didn't feel right when we met, I'd drive her to Kennedy Airport, and she'd go home to California.

That evening, I shaved every hour. I shaved at 1:00 A.M., 2:00 A.M. . . . Morning finally arrived. At 10:45 A.M., I put down the razor, got into my car, and with my housekeeper in tow, I drove to Terre's hotel. "Shirley," I said, "you stay double-parked down here. I don't know what's going to happen. Don't move."

I went up to the desk clerk: "Excuse me, I want to see Miss Blair. Don't call up."

And the guy says, "She's in room 1104, but she's checking out. I'm getting her bill ready."

And I'm thinking to myself, Oh, my God! She's made up her mind already. I can't let this happen. As I rode the elevator to her floor, part of me was so wildly anxious to see her at last; the other part feared that this might be the first and last time I would set eyes on her. To be honest, I looked sharp in my English blue suit and topcoat. If I knew how to smoke a pipe, it would have been the perfect touch. I arrived at the door of her room at precisely eleven.

But before I can press the doorbell, I see a piece of paper taped to the door. What's this? I thought. It's a handwritten questionnaire. The questions were (1) Do you think the person behind this door is wonderful? (2) Do you think the person behind this door really cares about you? (3) How do you spell her first name? (This was a trick question, since Terre spells her name with a final "e," not an "i" or "y." To this day, I wonder what would have happened if I had spelled it with a "y.") I filled out the questionnaire and slipped it under the door. And then I heard that familiar voice: "You can come in."

The door opened at a forty-five-degree angle. I still couldn't see her as she stood behind it. I simply said:

"Listen, I just want to ask you one question—it will have a lot to do with our future. Sight unseen, will you marry me?"

And she said, "Yes."

And then she closed the door. With me on the inside.

That's when I first saw her. She was beautiful: blond hair, green eyes—and a knockout smile. But more important, she was as warm as she sounded on the phone, open and lively and, in her own way, clearly as crazy as I was to be doing this. As minutes became hours, I realized more and more that the voice on the other end of the line for all these months would be my wife. Forever, and after that. We just looked at each other, holding hands, and sat down on the couch. We didn't want to unlock our hands. We drove out to my (now "our") house in Westhampton. (By now, Shirley had left the driving to us.) We had turkey sandwiches, the best smoked turkey sandwiches you've ever tasted. You might think I would have wined and dined Terre on caviar, pheasant under glass, flickering candles, all that romantic stuff. But I knew I didn't have to impress Terre or put on a show for her. Besides, these were the *best* turkey sandwiches in the world. I had them sent over by taxi from Southampton. So, if you're ever in the Hamptons and you want a fantastic turkey sandwich, check out the Golden Pear.

Shortly after sunset, we went upstairs to the bedroom. I put some logs on the fire. The reflection of the flames were sparkling in Terre's eyes. As we nestled closer to each other, it struck both of us at once: We felt sorry for Ma Bell's stockholders. There'd be no huge phone bill tonight. (And I didn't whisper, "I really need you," with the emphasis on the "really." I didn't have to say it. Terre knew.)

As the days passed, the best part was that there were no surprises along the way. Terre was everything I thought she would be. There didn't seem to be any skeletons in her closet. With the tons of clothes she had, how could there be?

I knew this was it, but I wasn't taking any chances. I wanted to make it official. I wanted to get married right away. But who would marry us this quickly? Terre knew how much my mother had meant to me, and she knew that I wanted to be married by a rabbi. And it was typical of Terre to be understanding and to tell me that if that's what I really wanted, it was all right with her. But I couldn't find a rabbi who would marry us this quickly. Terre has the capacity to make molehills out of mountains: "I know a rabbi who'll marry us." Terre, it turned out, with her interest in all religions, had taken courses with different religious teachers. One of them was Rabbi Joseph Gelberman. He married us in a private service on March 6, 1989.

The wedding was held downtown in the bowels of New York City in a minuscule temple, one of the tiniest places I'd ever seen. I wondered during the ceremony if I would have been as tolerant had she wanted to be married by a priest or minister? I hope so. My parents had both died by now, but I know they were there to watch us get married. And they loved it. I just know it.

Had it been left to Terre, she would have said that the private service was enough. But then it hit me: Marvin Hamlisch is a married man. Marvin Hamlisch has a wife. (Marvin Hamlisch doesn't have as much closet space.) Marvin Hamlisch gets a brand-new idea, he wants to celebrate.

I had never taken the time to celebrate anything in my life—not my Oscars or my Tonys or anything—and finding Terre seemed the best reason in the world. So I kept begging: "Sweetheart, I know you married an old, steadfast man of traditional values. And the wedding we had couldn't have been more perfect. But because of you, and us, there's a new me. And just for the delight of it, I want to share this: I want to see you come down the aisle in a gown, the most beautiful bride in modern history; I want to see your mother enjoy it; your family and my family and friends. Let's hear some trumpets in B-flat. Let's hear a heavenly choir sing out: '*Marvin Hamlisch is ready to be happy. Hallelujah!*'"

Terre resisted at first. She didn't want a big wedding. But she finally gave in to the mad composer. So we scrapped the honeymoon and started to plan for wedding number two, the one for the in-laws, friends, nephews, the cousins, and, of course, the aunts. The wedding with the big band without Marvin Hamlisch conducting.

We decided that we wanted to have the reception at Tavern on the Green, that sparkling restaurant in Central Park. We chose May 29 and bet on the fact that it would be a gorgeous summer day. We went over all the details with the restaurant and signed on the dotted line. But wait . . . you got it . . . here comes Hamlisch's Law again. Out of nowhere, Tavern on the Green was hit by a wildcat employees' strike. We started to panic, but the manager kept calling us, reassuring us:

"Mr. and Mrs. Hamlisch, don't worry about a thing. As God is my witness, we'll settle. I promise you we'll settle."

The strike continued. We panicked when we saw the picture of the picket line in the *Daily News*. The telephone rang:

"Mr. and Mrs. Hamlisch, this is Mr. Phillippe again from Tavern on the Green. Don't worry about a thing. As God is my witness, we'll settle. I promise you we'll settle." Either because we were half insane or so much in love, we took Mr. Phillippe at his word and sent out the invitations.

Two weeks before the wedding date and the strike wasn't over yet. Not only was the strike not settled, but it was getting ugly. Diners were getting slammed with eggs. There was a powerful, angry union involved here. Meanwhile, I had arranged for the Marine Corps Band, with their beautiful Strolling Strings, to play at our wedding. I may not know a lot about soldiering, but I knew enough to know that the Marine Corps Band was not about to cross a picket line. Neither were half our guests. The time had come for Terre and me to face up to reality and find another place. We were very distraught by now. I remember we were walking down Fifth Avenue and decided the one thing we didn't want was a big commercial hotel. We were standing in front of a travel agency, and my eye caught a breathtaking photograph of a fleet of sailboats. And then Terre said: "Marvin, I've always thought it would be great to get married on a ship."

Now one of the rare things about Terre, and it amazes me to this day, is how she can put a positive spin on almost anything. She had me convinced on the spot, right there on Fifth Avenue, that a wedding on a yacht could all be put together in two weeks—and furthermore, that the Tavern on the Green strike was a blessing in disguise. "Marvin, just think of the blue sky, the ocean water, out in the open. We'd be closer to God." I'll never forget her broad, beaming smile. Me, I was a wreck.

Yachts? What did I know about them? I didn't have a clue about how to find one. But then I had a wild idea. What could I lose? I looked up the phone numbers of the offices of Malcolm Forbes and Donald Trump. I hardly knew either of them, but I knew enough about them to know they owned yachts. The Malcolm Forbes office seemed to have a switchboard that was perpetually busy. I was luckier with Donald Trump, and although he said: "Sorry, Marvin, mine's not available on the twenty-ninth," he was kind enough to recommend the World Yacht Club. "I'm sure they'll have the right one for your wedding." Terre met with their staff to prepare the menu, the seating, and the whole order of events. So far, so good. But now, of course, we had to phone two hundred and fifty guests and tell them the new site of the reception.

May twenty-ninth arrived. It turned out to be a glorious sun-baked afternoon. The ceremony took place on dockside under an enormous tent. A few minutes before the ceremony, I put on my brand-new tuxedo. But wouldn't you know, a button fell off. For the first time all day, I got nervous. I made a frantic search. But thankfully, one of the marines in the Strolling Strings always carried needle and thread. (She also always carried a hand grenade.)

Terre, escorted by her brother Ron and looking like an angel, glided down the aisle to the music of Leonard Bernstein. I had to agree that playing the entire score of *A Chorus Line* would have taken too long. The rest, like an opening night, was a daze. But I still somehow remember the effervescence of Terre's mother, Marie, and her sister Charlotte. I remember my own sister, Terry, the sense of relief on her face that I had finally gotten married. I remember the wondrous sense of abandon, mixed with an avalanche of giggles, coming from my sweet nephew David Liebling. And ah, yes, the ever-present Richard Kagan, beaming from ear to ear, knowing that he would soon be writing one helluva life insurance policy.

The wedding was memorable. How could I ever forget it? For a year I kept paying the bills. Each week another bill would arrive. The florist. "Are you sure we needed that many flowers?" I said to Terre. (Here I was chafing over the bill for the flowers, the same guy who sent a ton of them during the courtship. Thus, the transformation from lover to husband.)

I had planned our honeymoon meticulously. As you know by now, I'm a guy who likes to leave nothing to chance. No surprises. I wanted the dream vacation, and that meant going to the South of France to the Hôtel du Cap. I had heard through the rumor mill that only God could afford a suite there. But what the heck. We had the airline tickets, we had the reservations, the passports, everything. It had gone like clockwork. And as we stood in the hotel lobby at three-thirty on a shining afternoon in June, I looked up at a tiny, hand-engraved plaque, in French, no less: "*On n'accepte pas American Express.*" Having taken French for five semesters, I struggled a bit but finally figured out the meaning of "*n'accepte pas.*" In an instant, I'm deranged. I only have a few traveler's checks, and I never carry much cash. I counted on my trusty American Express credit card. When they tell you not to leave home without it, sometimes you might as well.

So Terre and I grabbed a taxi and zoomed to the nearest American Express Bank. This was a Friday, and the place was about to close. Had this happened to Marvin, the lonely bachelor, I would have gone into one of my patented tirades. I would have lost control, which would not solve the problem but would make me feel a lot better. But now I was married. I could not embarrass my wife with a temper tantrum. I was a man with responsibilities. So did I scream at the teller when he tried to close his booth on us? Did I shout and demand to be served? Did I holler that I must have enough money to begin my magical honeymoon? You're damn right, I did.

"You must meet my wife," says the lovesick fellow in *A Little Night Music.* "Yes, I must, I really must . . ." replies his former lover, bored with the idea. But wait, give me a minute. I'd really like to tell you about my wife and my marriage. Usually, if you are describing a movie or a play you can say, "Well, it's like . . ." You can always draw a comparison. But Terre is like nobody I have ever met. She has a deep sense of right and wrong. That, coupled with a very spiritual bent and a great deal of compassion. She always stands up for the underdog. She fights for the issues she believes in, whether or not they are popular. She's not petty or gossipy. Some women I've known, their motto is "If you can't say something nice about a person, come sit by me." Not Terre. And all of this is enveloped by a childlike quality in her—in the way that a child knows what's right and what's wrong instinctively. Kids can smell hypocrisy. And that's Terre. She has no time for pretentiousness or dishonesty.

We were married for just a little while when Terre announced to me that she had decided, unilaterally, that she wouldn't go back to her television career. "When you go on the road, I can go with you. I'm tired of having to worry about juggling our schedules." But don't for a moment think that just because Terre gave up her career that she's now at home, polishing Marvin's piano. *Au contraire.* (That's five semesters' worth, all right.) She's a doer, a learner, an explorer. And you won't find her shopping all day long on Rodeo Drive or Madison Avenue. When it comes to *my* foibles—and believe me, they are many—she is the first to push me to the wall and make me realize where I have gone wrong. She can set me straight real quick.

People may rightfully have wondered about the circumstances of our telephone courtship, and they may even have questioned the soundness of our minds. You tell me, do you know anybody else who asked someone they had never seen to marry them? But the truth is, I was blessed with an exceptional ear, and what I heard in Terre's voice during those marathon phone calls was a woman who was straightforward, giving, and carefree. I heard the sound of an incredible woman who accepted me "as is." I knew I wouldn't have to play the piano for her, write songs for her, or even be a success. She liked me the way I was.

* * *

Early in our marriage, I said to Terre: "I want to take you to places you've never been." I expected she'd say, "Take me back to the South of France or to Venice or to Greece." Instead, she said, "I've always wanted to meet the Dalai Lama." If that's what my wife wants, that's what we've got to do. I'm a married man. So I dutifully call Tibet House in New York and ask if it's possible to meet the Dalai Lama. They give me the phone number of a woman named Michelle Bohana in Washington. She tells me the only way you can meet the Dalai Lama is to go to the town of Dharmsala in India, where he lives. She says if we manage to get there and stay for three days, he will grant us an audience.

Like the solicitous, demented husband I am, I phone Dharmsala and speak to someone and make all the arrangements. To get there, you have to fly from New York to New Delhi. From there you take another plane to a town called Jammu, which is on the Pakistani-Indian border. From there you travel for five hours in a small van or ox cart to the town of Dharmsala.

Getting to New Delhi was no problem. What we didn't know was that the five-hour car trip to Dharmsala was a bit hazardous. It was not like driving to Cape Cod. At the time, skirmishes were being fought on the border between Pakistan and India, and a miniwar was in progress. It was a volatile, explosive situation, very nearly as dangerous as your average New York subway. There were pitched battles being fought. And Terre and I, the innocents abroad, had come with a host of valises, gallons of Evian water, cases of toilet paper. Better we should have brought bulletproof vests.

We were on the road for maybe an hour when we reached a military checkpoint. Uh-oh. The soldiers were kids, about seventeen, looking proud of their nifty new machine guns.

And they decided they'd better check us out. You can't have a composer slipping behind your lines. So they prod us out of our car and make me open the valises. And I'm getting more frightened by the minute. Suddenly a guy puts his automatic weapon to my head and I'm thinking: Oh, my God—oh, my God. Here I am, on a pilgrimage to meet a great man of peace and I'm about to be blown to bits.

With the gun barrel at my head, I turned to Terre for what I thought might be the last time and whispered: "I don't think they know I wrote *A Chorus Line* here."

Miraculously we escaped with our lives and our Evian water. A few days later, we were summoned to an audience with the Dalai Lama. His serenity and graciousness were remarkable, and in many ways he filled us with inspiration. It was an experience I would never forget, and it's made me continually aware of the monumental tragedy of the Tibetans.

A few months after we returned from India, Terre looked at me and said:

"Marvin, it's time you knew that you're made up of more than your work. You never had a normal childhood, and you never knew what it meant to be happy when you were young. Tell me the truth: What was the one thing you really loved when you were growing up?"

"I was a baseball freak since I was a kid."

"Marvin, who did you root for?"

"It was the Yankees all the way."

Three weeks later I wake up to find a handsome brochure on my desk. Could it possibly say what I think it says: "Yankee Fantasy Camp." The whole thing had been arranged. It was a done deal; I was registered. "Yankee Fantasy Camp" is a place where *mature men* go to have their dreams come true. They go to Florida and play baseball with the stars of their youth—Mickey Mantle and Whitey Ford and the rest. One of the first musicals I saw as a teenager was *Damn Yankees*. In it the manager says, "A long-ball hitter, that's what we need. I'd sell my soul for a long-ball hitter."

So there I go—the kid who had been called "Fingers" Hamlisch. The kid who wanted to catch a fastball but couldn't, for fear of ending his career, was on his way to Florida, wife in hand, like a scene out of *Field of Dreams*. And I'm doing all the things I never had done as a child. Because, back then, as the kids were whipping the ball around the infield, I was home practicing the scales. And I'm thinking I might be meeting that great contemporary philosopher, Yogi Berra, who once said, "You can observe a lot by watching." And one of the things I'm observing is that the *players and coaches are nervous* and keep telling me: "Listen, Marv, if a ball's hit to you on a line and you don't think you can handle it, don't hurt your hands, don't break the hands that feed you—let it go." And I'm thinking: Are you kidding? I've been waiting for this all my life.

So armed with Mineral Ice and Ben-Gay, I started to play ball. A real jock. Pride of the Yankees. All these famous former baseball stars are telling me, "I'll never forget the night I saw *Chorus Line*," and I'm saying to them, "I'll never forget the catch you made against the Red Sox."

The great moment came for me in a game in which I got a single off Whitey Ford. It was unbelievable. Mickey Mantle was umpiring at second base. The next batter came up and hit a single, and I should have gone to third base, but I stopped at second. The coach kept signaling me to make the turn and take third. But I stayed planted at second. When the inning was over, John Blanchard, the coach, stormed over to me: "Why the hell did you stop at second? Why didn't you take third? Weren't you watching the damn sign?"

"I'll tell you the truth," I said. "I couldn't. I couldn't leave second base. How could I? It's not every day I get a chance to talk to Mickey Mantle."

So remember, folks, if you ever come across the highly regarded best-seller *Famous Jewish Sports Legends*, look under "H" for Hamlisch.

Indulge me in two more stories that probably wouldn't have happened if I were still an unmarried man. These are musical stories, but they're not the kind you might be expecting. They are about two original works that I came to write unlike anything I had done before. No, it was not Broadway, and it was not Hollywood. But I was itching to experiment, and it was astounding to me that I had taken so many years to see that I had actually been restricted by music. Now, in this new phase of my life, I was revved up to explore new musical forms. So whatever the outcome, I consider these adventures critical to my evolution as a composer.

The first story goes more or less like this: One day in the summer of 1990 I received a phone call from Dallas, a city I knew well from my concert tours. The man on the phone was Liener Temerlin, whom I had met in Texas and who had been introduced to me by John Green, one of the truly great composers and arrangers of cinema music.

"Marvin, there's a woman down here named Wendy Reves. Her late husband was Emery Reves. He was a close friend of Winston Churchill's. He also wrote a book called *The Anatomy of Peace*." Then Liener sprang it on me: "For years, Wendy has been looking for a composer to set the theme of this book to music. She wants to honor her late husband and have the piece premiere with the Dallas Symphony Orchestra. Marvin, I've suggested you to Wendy for this."

Of course, I always knew that I had an unfinished symphony in me—not that I ever started one.

"Why not?" I told Liener. "If I could write 'Sunshine, Lollipops and Rainbows,' I can write a symphony." I ordered two reams of music paper, cleared my desk, got a dozen brand-new pens, rolled up my sleeves, and was ready to go.

I thought I could make Reves's theme—that most of the world's countries "are caught up in their own nationalism"—work by having the orchestra represent the world itself. I would begin with loud, dissonant uproar. (Incidentally, Albert Einstein, who was a great champion of Reves, had agreed that we were all too "nationalistic, competitive, and separative." Einstein went on to talk about the grave danger of national prejudices that serve "to make us citizens of our nations but not the world.") Suddenly, I could hear coming out of the wildness one solo flute introducing a plaintive theme, beckoning the nations. This melody would act as a magnetic force, pulling in each section of the orchestra, one by one.

Yet there was still something missing. The orchestra alone wasn't enough. I stared at the blank paper. Nothing came. Even more agony. I was exhausted. I looked out at the trees, heard the birds, and thought about the Ben & Jerry's in the freezer. Some things never change. The roadblock was that I had to find the right structure for the piece. Having choices, for once, I discovered, can be more difficult than writing to formula. It was time to distance myself from all this, and I think almost two months went by. Then something curious happened: late one night I heard the theme, but this time it was leading *me* and not the other way around. I started following. My pen seemed to be going down a road that was predetermined, and I was led to the discovery that what I needed was the human voice. The voice of a child.

* * *

I was excited about this in a new way. It had taken eight months, but it had all come together. I wish my father had been alive to know that his son had his concerto at last. I knew my old friend Lorin Hollander would understand how I felt, and so I called him.

"Lorin, how are you? You won't believe what I've been up to. I've never told you, but I was commissioned to write a symphony six months ago, and I've just finished it."

"I wish your father were alive," Lorin said.

"I was just thinking the same thing."

"Why don't you come over tomorrow night with Terre so I can hear it? But there's a book I want you to look at—promise me you'll read it right away. I'll send it over by messenger."

Sure enough, the next morning I received a paperback called *Lexicon of Musical Invective*, by Nicolas Slonimsky. The subtitle? "Critical Assaults on Composers Since Beethoven's Time." I flipped through the pages:

> We find Beethoven's Ninth Symphony to be precisely one hour and five minutes long; a fearful period indeed, which puts the muscles and lungs of the orchestra, and the patience of the audience, to a severe trial. . . .
>
> —*The Harmonicon*, London, April 1825

Then I thought I'd see how Tchaikovsky would fare:

> Tchaikovsky's First Piano Concerto, like the first pancake, is a flop. . . .
>
> —Nicolai Soloviev, *Novoye Vremya*,
> St. Petersburg, November 13, 1875

I thought I'd try one of our modern greats, George Gershwin:

> How trite and feeble and conventional the tunes are [in Gershwin's *Rhapsody in Blue*]. How sentimental and vapid the harmonic treatment, under its disguise of fussy and futile counterpoint. . . . [One cannot but] weep over the lifelessness of the melody and harmony, so derivative, so stale, so inexpressive!
>
> —Lawrence Gilman, *New York Tribune*, February 13, 1924

Good old Lorin, he was trying to protect me from what he knew could be a hazardous trial by fire.

Rehearsals went well in Dallas, though there were changes to be made. Maestro Edoardo Mata, the conductor, was both brilliant and helpful, fully understanding what I wanted the piece to convey and in total control of how to get that message across. Sink or swim, this was twenty-eight minutes of nothing but music by Marvin Hamlisch. In truth, I was a nervous wreck.

On the night of the performance, the first half of the program featured Beethoven's *Eroica* Symphony. Well, at least I was in good company, although I couldn't recall what the reviews in Slonimsky said about this one. After what seemed like a very long intermission, it was time for *Anatomy of Peace*. The orchestra tuned up, the houselights dimmed, the conductor mounted the podium, and I grabbed Terre's hand.

The audience settled down. It began, just as I had envisioned it over a year ago—the driving beginning with its harsh sounds of discord. And then that theme of the flute. That simple, haunting, straightforward melody that I had sought out among all those notes on the keyboard. Now it was realized by a masterful flutist; she made each note glide gently. The rhythmic brass section zoomed in, with Maestro Mata capturing the syncopated feel of it. He pushed the orchestra to pick up the rhythm. He quieted things down as the theme was restated, but this time joined by the rest of the woodwinds. The flute was picking up allies, and the cello solo, exquisite in tone, was a stunning highlight. Now the brass succumbed, and finally the strings.

Then, out of nowhere, the voice of a child. The suddenness of his entrance was startling. The orchestra became contemplative, echoing the words of the soloist. There was a rousing, triumphant finale as the music crescendoed to the embrace of the main theme. I prayed I had done justice to Emery Reves's message. That was for others to decide. But I knew that I had written *Anatomy of Peace* with my own convictions, my own passion. I wrote it the way I did because I wanted to. And if nothing else, that night in Dallas was the way I would have to approach all of my music from then on.

The second story goes like this. Terre and I are having breakfast. I'm having carrot juice, oat bran cereal, bran muffins, followed by a daily dose of vitamins served up with a large glass of Evian water. (Where's a good deli when you need it?)

Terre is reading the newspaper. She seems to be taken by something and looks up at me with her girlish grin.

"I know what the world needs," she says.

"I see," I say.

She tells me she's serious about this: "It's what *Anatomy of Peace* was all about. It all fits together," she says. She tells me it's in these articles every day. "Look at the Berlin Wall. Look at the collapse of communism. We're actually on our way to becoming a global community." I look at her.

"We need a new kind of song."

"What?"

"We need an anthem for everyone."

For a moment, I didn't get it, but then, slowly, the idea started growing on me. I liked it. But I couldn't help wondering how any lyricist would react to a phone call from me asking: "Hi, wanna write an anthem today?" Of course, two years ago I would have never even thought of writing a symphony, so the idea of writing an anthem wasn't as farfetched as it sounded. I called Alan and Marilyn Bergman in Los Angeles. If anyone would understand, they would.

"We'll get back to you," they said. I guess I hadn't set them on fire. But sure enough, two weeks later, they sent me two verses. And the opening line: "If we all sing One Song." We started faxing each other, exchanging cassettes, and running up the Federal Express bill. From the start, I saw this as a chance to take the message of *Anatomy of Peace* and extend it vocally into a popular song. The major hurdle to writing an anthem for today is to keep it from sounding overblown, funereal, and predictably old-fashioned. I wanted an anthem that was contemporary and spoke to the times we live in. I wanted to capture the new spirit that came with the end of the cold war and the triumph of democracy—I had learned from Leonard Bernstein that music must reach out to the political issues of our times. I think I am correct in saying that he felt that any composer who failed to do this was not living up to the true spirit of the gift he had been given. I kept thinking about the lyric from the Bergmans, particularly the line "Imagine what tomorrow would bring / if we all sing / One Song." And that was exactly the challenge. A child in Nigeria should be able to feel the music as his own as much as a child in Tokyo, Moscow, or Prague.

I actually saw this come true. In 1990, "One Song" had its premiere at Carnegie Hall with Barbara Cook as soloist accompanied by the United Nations Children's Chorus, dressed in their native garb, representing more than fifty-two of the nations of the world. The following day, the Bergmans called. They had heard how well our song had gone over.

"Marvin, we've got to take this further. I think this is for Quincy Jones."

We knew how committed he was to world brotherhood. If he was interested, he would tell us right away. If he wasn't, he wouldn't lie about it. That much is sure about Quincy. I sent him a tape. About two weeks later, he called me: "Marvin, this is the right song for the right time. But you have to be patient. 'One Song' needs international exposure. And I've just got to find the right venue, which could take some time. Don't worry, I won't let you down."

And Quincy, bless him, came through. He brought "One Song" to the 1992 Olympics in Barcelona. It was heard by over one billion people.

It's obvious by now that I took to married life like my agent to his commission. But the question arises: How do I rate myself as husband material? Frankly, I'm not the easiest person in the world to live with. As you already know, this book is a bible of my eccentricities. High on the list of my worst traits is that I can be very scattered, like a jigsaw puzzle unsolved. Or I can be very funny, particularly in the morning, off the wall, with an excess of energy. I still don't know why Terre finds it odd that I wake up at 6:00 A.M., get into my blue robe, carrying my muffin and orange juice, and then wake her up singing "the news of the day," inspired by the latest headlines in the *New York Times*.

> Terre, the economy's gettin' lame—
> Bush is after Saddam Hussein—
> Yeltsin refuses to take the blame—
> And Congress is bouncin' checks *agayne*!

Isn't this the way the rest of America wakes up? I know, that's a lot to take that early. But mercifully, instead of trying to change me, Terre stoically accepts those twenty-minute "musicales" because she knows that when the madness has subsided, it's going to be smooth sailing. Remember those headaches I used to get so often? They're gone. Somehow or other, almost magically, she is the antidote to that disease. I am no longer depressed. She has taught me that depression is wasted energy, that it's stealing time from the best moments of our relationship.

Now, let me clue you in. Before you start feeling sorry for Terre, understand that her taking me exactly as I am has made me: (1) an ardent husband, (2) faithful, (3) concerned, (4) steadfast, (5) adoring, (6) happy at home, (7) more open to vegetarian cuisine, (8) a man who actually bought a Maltese dog, (9) a person who gets on a treadmill, (10) a man who gave up three of his shelves in the bathroom, (11) a man who actually likes a fireside when a storm is due, potato chips, moonlight, and motor trips, (12) a man who is a devoted husband and is actually married to the wife he is devoted to, (13) a man who is opening up new vistas without the help of a set designer, (14) an artist who is faithful and very much in love with someone other than himself, (15) a man who can finally recall some of the *good* things the critics have said about him.

And as a Romeo, Woody Allen has nothing on me.

Thank you, sweetheart.

12.

BEGINNINGS

Too bad no one took a snapshot of me mulching in our garden in the back of our house on Long Island. They probably wouldn't believe it, anyway. I can hardly believe it myself. Not only was I mulching, but I was in no particular hurry. After all, I was in love, and for the first time I was allowing myself to rethink what kind of person I was and wanted to be. One of the things I found out about marriage, which was unexpected, was that it makes it much easier to look at one's life and reassess oneself. When you are alone, you are actually more likely to find yourself obsessing about yourself. I used to go round and round in circles to the point where I had locked myself into myself—by myself. But having someone to be with all the time, to talk to about everything, unlocks a lot of closed doors. It is easier to get to know oneself more clearly when you have a sounding board or someone who can reflect a mirror image back to you. The constant give-and-take is so easy and spontaneous.

This is all the more invaluable because marriage had come to me so late. I had spent all of my youth and formative years focused on work and success. There'd been room for nothing else. It had all started innocently enough: when I sat down at our Sohmer upright on West Eighty-first Street at the age of five, all I knew was that music was easy for me. I heard sounds that other children didn't hear. Juilliard, for better or for worse, exposed me to a world of competitiveness, and once I had seized on that, I was on a collision course that nearly destroyed me. It was Queens College at 7:30 A.M., the taxis back to the city for *The Bell Telephone Hour*, the knocking on door after door in the Brill Building, the film scores, *The Way We Were* and *The Sting*. And then—*A Chorus Line*. Now I had even more to live up to. What would be my next *Chorus Line*? It became a question of building more hotels on Boardwalk, not realizing that life had a few custard pies up its sleeve.

But for all my early triumphs and being way ahead of my years professionally, I had never matured enough emotionally. Success fed on success, but it was a vicious cycle. And I do remember sensing, somewhere within me, that I had to find a way out of being alone—not merely a relationship for relationship's sake, but a relationship with someone intuitive and centered. For all the show business in me, and there's enough, I have always remained anchored to the beliefs my parents imbued in me. Lilly and Max were not mere figures in a childhood family drama. They had a lasting effect, and they laid a very deep emotional foundation. Maybe it was too difficult to live up to, which might explain why there were detours and mistakes. I realize now that I came to confuse success with being true to oneself, sharing enough with others, knowing what was really right for me. Maybe that's why it was so important for me to visit Miss Goldstein in the hospital. She had unalterable values in that cubicle of a classroom. She was true to herself; and she never wavered from that.

* * *

I am continually finding new realities for me. There has been a lot I had to accept that I have never faced up to. The pain of losing Michael Bennett and Ed Kleban, the fact that I had been scared to go on without them, that I could never bring myself to admit: "They're gone, Marvin, and they took some of you with them." That I kept looking for some magical lifeline to be thrown to me so that I could grab it as it brought me back to shore. I had always expected that some *deus ex machina* would arrive to rescue me. Only now am I coming to see that for years I have been looking in the wrong place—that I have been looking outside instead of *inside*. My life has stopped being about "showing them." It has started to be about showing me. For in truth, I now have options. It no longer has to be great hit, greater hit, greatest hit.

I've come to see that music can make a difference, that it can reach hundreds of millions of people in an instant, that it can share new ideas, that in some cases it can actually effect social change. It's been nineteen years since I wrote the music for *The Way We Were*, and now, after all that time, Barbra and I were reunited again—with our dear friends Alan and Marilyn Bergman. It was for a song we had written called "Common Threads," performed in the very political year of 1992 in Los Angeles as a rallying cry for the women of America and for the women of the world. I see now that the uses of music go way beyond what I do myself, sitting at my piano.

Now I know where real rewards in music can be for me. I can see a lot of new beginnings. It's different now. I've come to surrender the need for success. Which is not to say that I would ever abandon Broadway or that I don't have one or two new musicals in my head. Neil Simon and I have been talking about one of them for the last six months. And so have David Hwang (author of *M. Butterfly*) and I over the last year. Who knows?

Emerson once said that "every man is a consumer, and ought to be a producer. He fails to make his place good in the world unless he not only pays his debt but also adds something to the common wealth." I take these words as my inspiration now, and I devoutly wish that I will leave something behind and pay my musical debt.

I go back, perhaps almost daily, to one of the most important conversations of my life. I didn't realize then that Michael Bennett and I were really talking not only about Broadway but about life itself. Because these simple words have taken on more and more meaning for me as I keep learning more and more about myself:

"Marvin, do you think you've done good work?"

"Yes."

"Do you love what you've done?"

"Yes."

"Do you think you wasted any of your time?"

"No."

"Then that's all you can do."

IMAGE GALLERY

Marvin Hamlisch and Terre Blair married on May 29, 1989, on a New York riverfront pier before 300 guests. Marvin composed and sang a special "wedding song" to his new bride: "Life is waiting, Terre, it's time, loving you is so easy to do."

Marvin was a life-long devoted fan of the New York Yankees. In November, 1989, he was one of 78 "campers" who attended the New York Yankees fantasy baseball camp in Fort Lauderdale, Florida, run by Mickey Mantle and other former players.

Marvin was appointed the Baltimore Symphony Orchestra's first Principal Pops Conductor in 1996, a post he retained for four years. He was beloved by Baltimore audiences for his irrepressible onstage wit and creative programming, and by musicians for his remarkable musicianship and infectious enthusiasm. Joseph Meyerhoff Symphony Hall, Baltimore, Maryland, 1997. Photo courtesy of the Baltimore Symphony Orchestra.

Marvin and Terre at the Kennedy Center Honors Reception with President Clinton, December 7, 1997. The former president characterized Marvin as "A goodhearted, humble and hilarious genius" in his eulogy at New York's Temple Emanuel. White House photograph.

Marvin was the Principal Pops Conductor of the Pittsburgh Symphony Orchestra from 1995 until his death. While in town for a music event with the Pittsburgh Symphony, Marvin joined the cast of Pittsburgh Musical Theater's *A Chorus Line* at the Byham Theater, and shared his personal recollections about the groundbreaking musical that garnered him a Tony Award, Drama Desk Award, and Pulitzer Prize for Drama. January 17, 2003. Photo copyright 2003 Patti Brahim. Courtesy of the Pittsburgh Symphony Orchestra and Pittsburgh Cultural Trust.

Marvin was the Principal Pops Conductor of the National Symphony Orchestra from 2000 to 2011. During the 2004–2005 Pops series, Marvin phoned Santa Claus as elves stood by to run Christmas errands. The John F. Kennedy Center for the Performing Arts, Washington, DC. December 9, 2004. Copyright 2004 Carol Hollans Pratt, with the permission of the parents of Nathaniel M. Pratt, Laura Loy, and Emily C. Pratt.

Long-time friend Gregory Tucker interviewed Marvin about his life and music during a John Adams Institute event in The Hague, The Netherlands. September 19, 2011.

Finale of "One Singular Sensation: A Tribute to Marvin Hamlisch" during rehearsal, Pittsburgh Symphony Orchestra, Heinz Hall, January 29, 2013. Photo copyright 2013 Len Prince

TRIBUTES TO MARVIN HAMLISCH

President Bill Clinton

Rabbis, Terre, family and friends:

First, I thank you for giving me the chance to celebrate and give thanks for the life of a great, giving genius. He gave us all the gift of our memories and we remember him in different ways, which is why I could sense all over almost relief when the choir began to sing, because everyone then was free to celebrate his remarkable life through their own memories.

Genius is rare enough, but a good-hearted genius is rarer still. A good-hearted, humble, and hilarious genius—almost unheard of.

My own memories of Marvin come from the fact that he liked to say "yes" more than "no." And I can't tell you how many times over the last two decades he said yes to Hillary or to me, not just in campaigns but in the State Department, the White House, and the work of my Foundation. He always knew that his gift could empower other people and touch hundreds of thousands, even millions, of people because of what he did, often in a small room, wearing just a sport coat, sitting a couple of feet away from—not the grand audiences that give you Oscars and Emmys and Tonys and Pulitzer Prizes—but just people-stunned and happy as a clam to see this funny, giving genius.

In his memoir *The Way I Was*, he said that—and all the press quoted this, which I thought was great—that his highly demanding father said "Marvin, when Gershwin was your age, he had a concerto. Where is your concerto?" We are Marvin's concerto.

We are grateful that he was given to us for thirty more years than George Gershwin, and we are grateful to be small notes in a remarkable symphony.

So now, the final movement of his great symphony *The Way I Was* is clearly "Nobody Did it Better."

—President Bill Clinton

Terre Blair Hamlisch

Thank you, Mr. President, for your kind words (and I just heard from Hillary as well—please thank her).

I'd like to point out something first about today's choir: It's no ordinary choir. What started out as a small, simple choir, grew by the day, formed by already invited guests and musical colleagues. His peers have chosen to sing in this choir to honor Marvin. It's filled with renowned composers, it has singers like Lucie Arnaz, it has stellar orchestrators like Jonathan Tunick, and brilliant lyricists like Sheldon Harnick and Rupert Holmes. Marvin would be so pleased to be honored by his esteemed peers in this way. Thank you, Judy Clurman, for this amazing gift.

My name is Terre Blair Hamlisch. In the last several days, as in the last 24 years, I have learned just how right Marvin Hamlisch was in so much. In our home, when I admitted he was right about something, he would affectionately and jokingly say: "Could you say that louder, please?"

When he left to score the movie *Behind the Candelabra* he said: "I know my talents. And it's not that I think I am irreplaceable, but I do sort of have an experience and a voice to add to this project that is unique." Well, Marvin, you were wrong: You are not replaceable!—and the world is saying it loudly now. You were a genius, a giant in your field and as a human being. Quoting your friend Michael Keller: "The world is dimmer and a lot less funny without you."

There is a poverty of adjectives in expressing our sorrow for the loss of Marvin Hamlisch. There is only one Marvin Hamlisch in the world.

Marvin taught me how to live life with gusto and magic. He would order every dessert on the menu, so everyone could taste everything and miss nothing in life. His friend Lily gave him a luncheon in France and it was a luncheon that was only desserts. He dug into those desserts like he did life: with fearless abandon and unbridled joy and enthusiasm. His life force was huge. I, on the other hand, am more cautious by nature. He took my hand and he led me into his world of magic, where even the mundane became electrified with his humor, joy, laughter and brilliant insight. I remember when I would become totally confounded over an idea or behavior of his, and my good friend Jason Epstein at the time would say calmly: "Terre, you married a real bonafide genius, not a salesman; it's a different skills set."

And Jason would quietly list the characteristics of "genius" to help me understand: The childlike enthusiasm, the rarefied creativity, and of course, the quick brilliant mind.

Marvin was the most loyal and supportive friend imaginable. I don't know people like this. If I was sad or discouraged or had one of life's curve balls hit me, Marvin would jump on top of the bed—much before I would prefer to wake up, mind you—and perform an entire musical complete with lyrics and choreography and the dancing chorus, playing all the parts himself to the disbelief of myself and our dogs. But he always got me to laugh my way out of it. Marvin did the same for his close friend Liza—Liza, he loved you so!—When they were young, on subways, going to auditions, he would belt out in song to Liza: "You'll be swell! You'll be great!" from *Gypsy*, to cheer her up.

Marvin's generosity was unparalleled by anyone I have ever met or seen. If your child needed a doctor, he was there to help. He performed for families, for terminally ill people, friends, and the elderly lady next door. Marvin worked to keep arts in impoverished school systems. He always said to me: "I wonder if anyone realizes I never say no." He never said no, he was there and he kept giving. And this is important. He never told people all that he did. He did not brag. He did not boast. He was down to earth and never thought he was better than anyone else. Even at Campbell's Funeral Home were these stories that people told me in the last days—one story was about opening night of one of Marvin's musicals on Broadway, and out of everyone in the theatre, Marvin got up first to help a man who was choking. It was Marvin who ran for the water and comforted him.

As a human being his character was beyond great: he mentored thousands and thousands of young people and never boasted, and never bragged. So so much, that no one ever knew. That was true humility. Humility is such an interesting quality to have in this world today, and often overlooked, misinterpreted and under-appreciated, but a quality of a giant character. Marvin lived by his mother's 'Bambi' rule. When I would fly off about someone's petty injustice he would quote: "If you don't have anything nice to say about someone, don't say anything at all." He lived by that and saw the best in everyone. He had deep, wide compassion and understanding for their behavior and tons of forgiveness and love.

Marvin loved deeply, was sensitive, and passionate. His passion for music, especially for the theatre, was who he was. But he also had a boundless love and passion for his beloved Yankees and for his dear close friend Joe Torre. He used to have the Yankees' score whispered to him by someone strolling down stage right as he was performing. That's until he found this gizmo he bought that he could put on the conductor's stand. I thought I always sensed a bit more enthusiastic movement in "Rhapsody" if the Yankees were winning, but maybe that was just me.

Marvin said, "Music is the universal language that brings people together." After receiving thousands and thousands of e-mails from Japan, Australia, Italy, England, Switzerland,

Canada, Sweden, Korea, Germany, Austria, Israel and more, I know that what he believed and said was not idle rhetoric. The world is mourning the loss of Marvin Hamlisch. When I was a student at the School for International Training, my fellow students were from the worst war torn countries: Afghanistan, Sudan, Darfur, Iraq. And do you know what Marvin did? He hired buses and he bused all of my friends to see the musical *Fela!* He was always doing something for someone else.

As the genius process goes, sometimes he would write things that some people did not get right away. And he'd say, "It's okay, Terre, I will be known as the 'people's composer,' because I will make music accessible to lots and lots of people and give them joy."

Marvin saved cultural institutions; his leadership vision and contagious personality and enthusiasm from the stage transformed symphonies, symphonies that were in very difficult financial circumstances. And audiences adored him. He increased the Pasadena Symphony pre-sales 200% and had unprecedented sales. He saved cultural institutions, therefore continuing culture in our country. I liked the card on the Pasadena Symphony's flowers. It said: "Marvin was genius with genuineness." It was just to be announced this week that he would be the Philadelphia Orchestra Musical Pops Director. He had so many things he was looking forward to. His friend Jay Stein says he was the Steve Jobs of his industry. He started early and ended early. But he changed lives. Marvin had this quote hanging in front of his desk that he looked at every day. It's a quote from His Holiness, the 14th Dalai Lama. It says: "The true meaning of life: We are visitors on this planet. We are here for 90 or 100 years at the most. During that period, we must try to do something good, something useful with our lives. If you contribute to other people's happiness, you will find the true goal, the true meaning of life."

You did that, honey! You were so much greater than you ever

thought. How fortunate we all are that in our time you came our way. How incredibly lucky and grateful and honored and humbled I was to share 24 years with you. Thank you from the depths of my heart. I love you, Marvin, and I always will. Just like it said on our wedding napkins: "Forever and after that."

Thank you . . . Thank you from all of us.

—Terre Blair Hamlisch, wife of Marvin Hamlisch

Lily Safra

Dearest Terre, My Beloved Marvin,

I am here today to say thank you for all the happy moments you have given us. I want to remember only the wonderful times we have spent together.

All the holidays in the South of France . . . you, always with your exquisite smile, playing the piano and singing for us, making jokes, being so kind to my children and grandchildren, and mostly to Edmond and myself.

Now, you will join Edmond and be in peace together.

I shall never forget whenever you were in Washington, you always found the time to play and sing at the home that we built at The National Institutes of Health for the families of the patients who were being treated there. You gave them so many happy moments. You helped them forget all the suffering they were going through.

Marvin my friend, God knows how caring and marvelous you have been, the many hearts you have touched, and how much joy you brought to so many people around the world.

I was privileged to have you in my life.

Now, you are in heaven, my angel, and I know you will continue taking care of Terre and all of us who will never forget you.

Thank you, Marvin, for all our good times together.

May God bless you. I will always love you.

A bientôt.

—Lily Safra,
chairwoman, Edmond J. Safra Foundation

Sir Howard Stringer

Thirty seven years ago, *A Chorus Line* opened off Broadway. Three months later it moved to Broadway. If it wasn't an overnight sensation, it became one at that moment. Everyone who saw it tells you they discovered it and everyone wanted to see it again.

It was, looking back, the very first musical reality show . . . and it had a book, lyrics and music whose integrity, credibility and originality made it one of the greatest musicals of all time. It made Marvin a music legend. He deserved every accolade.

The reason, the extraordinary success of this Tony-winning, Pulitzer Prize–winning phenomenon didn't crush Marvin with the weight of future expectations is because, at heart, Marvin was—for all his critical success—simply the merriest of minstrels. He was happy in his own skin.

To be sure, Terre helped to keep him grounded, but he worked for fun. At opening night of the 2006 *Chorus Line* revival, Avery Corman, a friend of the late Ed Kleban—who wrote the lyrics for the show—went up to Marvin to congratulate him. Before he could speak, Marvin jumped in quickly, "Isn't it great to hear Ed's lyrics again?" Marvin's generosity of spirit was immediately evident. At a moment of triumph he was thinking of someone else . . . not himself.

You all know the litany of his musical successes—from "They're Playing Our Song" through "The Way We Were" and "Nobody Does It Better" to his newest Liberace compositions. Oscars, Tonys, Emmys, Grammys and Golden Globes are somewhere in his closet. Neither he nor Terre ever seemed to display them. There wasn't room for them on his piano anyway.

Marvin, a young prodigy, Marvin, the great composer. Marvin, the ubiquitous conductor. Marvin, the generous accompanist and arranger. Marvin, who created a body of work few can match.

But Marvin, the man. Marvin, the friend, is matchless in his own right. If there was an award for being a mensch, he'd have a ton of them.

As the first speaker, I could try to reprise his brilliant career, but there will be a memorial service before long with musicians and singers to echo his genius more appropriately. My sense of loss is too immediate, too painful. My memories of our private relations and the time spent with Terre and Marvin crowd out the public figure.

Many years ago, Marvin and Terre, my wife and I, began a tradition of throwing Christmas parties in my home for about thirty close friends. There was no space for any more. Since half the friends were Jewish, this was really a secular celebration of joyous music associated with Christmas.

Marvin transformed these evenings into his musical playground . . . words and arrangements by Marvin Hamlisch. The Twelve Days of Christmas was re-written to include the names of every single guest.

Two Turtle Doves became Barbara Walters. Three French Hens became Harry Evans. Four Calling Birds became 4 Peter Stones. And Five Golden Rings became Mort Zuckerman. He rewrote "We Three Kings of Orient Are" and dragged Sir David Frost, Sir Evelyn Rothschild and Sir Jeremy Greenstock in front of the guests to sing "We Three Knights of Great Britain Are . . ."

He got Nora Ephron to sing the rarely heard and singularly secular intro to White Christmas. You know it: "The Sun is shining, the Grass is Green, The Orange and Palm Trees sway. There's never been such a day. In Beverly Hills LA."

He played "We Wish you a Merry Christmas", in the manner of Andrew Lloyd Webber, then Mozart and Les Misérables. He followed that with a perfect impression of Johnny Mathis.

On one occasion, he got Michael Crawford, the original

Phantom of the Opera to sing "Oh Holy Night" without microphone. You could have heard a pin drop.

Unfortunately, word got out about these Christmas parties and we were bombarded with requests for invitations. There was no more room in our inn. We reluctantly canceled the event because we were disappointing so many friends. A month ago we talked about trying again but time ran out.

He was an amazing friend, loyal and generous. I remember he was invited to accept an award in Vienna, the first home of Marvin's parents before they were driven out in the Anschluss. He began his acceptance speech with a meaningful and revealing opening sentence. "My father," he said, "loved Vienna. He didn't want to leave." An honored guest making an important statement, graciously.

We all know how hard Marvin worked. He was composing to the end. Terre was there for him all the time wishing he would work less, but putting him back together so he could continue his search for the perfect melody, the perfect performance. Terre, you have been a remarkable, unselfish partner all these years.

I remember when you and I sat in the audience at a Barbara Streisand concert when Marvin was conducting. Whenever Marvin thought Barbra wouldn't notice, he would lean out and wave at us with that mischievous grin. The merry minstrel!

Terre, in this moment of profound sadness, try to picture the mischievous smile of an extraordinary man, loved by so many. And know that he loved you best! You are the minstrel's girl.

Yes, he loved you. He didn't want to leave.

—Sir Howard Stringer,
chairman of the Board of Directors of Sony Corporation

Rabbi Paul Kushner

We have gathered here this morning not because Marvin Hamlisch died, but because Marvin Hamlisch lived. Let this service be a celebration of his extraordinary life, as much as it is a collective expression of grief at his tragic and untimely passing. There is a story told in the Talmud: Rabbi Yochanan ben Zakkai, one of the great sages of 2000 years ago, one day called in his finest disciples, and gave them an extraordinary charge. He said to them: "Go out, leave this hall of academia, go into the villages, enter the marketplaces, observe people and come back and tell me what is the single most important quality for a person to have in this world." The disciples went out, they mingled, they observed, they trickled back. Rabbi Eliezer said, "ayin tova," a good outlook. If you have a good outlook on life you have everything. Rabbi Yosi said, "shachen tov," be a good neighbor. That's the essence of life. Rabbi Yoshua said "chaver tov," be a good companion. And finally Rabbi Eleazar ben Arach, destined to become one of the great sages of the next generation, returned and said two simple, monosyllabic Hebrew words, "Lev tov," a good heart. The elderly Rabbi Yochanan stroked his long white beard and smiled. And after a lengthy pause, he said, "Each of you have done well, but if I must choose one answer, I will select that of Rabbi Eleazar ben Arach who said 'a good heart.' Because his answer subsumes each of yours."

Ayin tov, a good outlook: Marvin had a wonderful outlook on life. He enjoyed life. He was always turned on. There were times we'd be alone, and I'd say to him "Marvin, relax. You're not performing now, it's just the two of us." And he would look at me as if to say: "This is how I relax." I shall arrogate to the other speakers the task of accounting his many achievements and his many awards that he received justly. Suffice to say, when I first met Marvin, he was fifteen years old. His mother said, "This is my son Marvin. Someday he will be the greatest composer in Hollywood." At the time it sounded like hubris. In retrospect I must say, she underestimated him. He became the greatest composer in Hollywood and on Broadway, as well as a great pianist, conductor and performer. And yet for all of his greatness, he remained close to—dare I use the phrase—*the common people*. There was one time we had gone to an exhibit at the Metropolitan Museum, and while we were admiring the works of art, two matronly women with Southern dialects called me over and said: "When you're alone with Mr. Hamlisch, please tell him how very much we appreciate his music." I said, "Oh, would you like to meet him? Marvin, come here! You have two fans." He came over, he chatted with them, he signed their programs. He made their day. For them it was an extraordinary moment. For Marvin it was typical.

Many years ago I read an article about an Indian tribe in Patagonia in The Argentine that has a very rich native language, with very beautiful idioms. And in this Patagonian language when one takes leave of a very, very dear friend, he doesn't just say "goodbye" or "see you around." He says: "I like myself better when I am with you." Marvin had that quality. You didn't just enjoy him, you liked yourself better when you were with him. That is a beautiful outlook on life.

Shachen tov, a good neighbor: This world is a better place because Marvin was in it. His sense of humor was as all encompassing as was his musical talent. The story is told in the Talmud of a great rabbi of the third century, Rabbi Berachiah, who one day was in the marketplace and he met Elijah the prophet. The fact that Elijah had been dead for thousands of years didn't throw him. He knew that Elijah walks the earth and Elijah knows past, present and future. Rabbi Berachiah asked Elijah: "Who is there here who will be my roommate in the world to come?" Elijah pointed to a street entertainer, a juggler, a comedian. Rabbi Berachiah was taken aback and said: "A clown? I am the greatest scholar of the age. I shall spend eternity with a clown? What has he done to deserve that great honor?" And Elijah the prophet said: "He makes people laugh." It can be said of Marvin: he made people laugh.

He was extraordinarily generous, not just in obvious ways, but in little ways. Whenever we would visit him, we had to be very careful to refrain from admiring something too enthusiastically. He would insist on giving it to us, not because he didn't want it, but because he wanted to make us happy. He tutored many young musicians—without charge, it wasn't a professional thing—but because he loved people, and loved music. And whenever one of his students would become famous, and several did, Marvin regarded the individual as a new colleague, and never as a competitor. Shachen tov, he was the quintessential good neighbor.

Chaver tov: a good companion. As he loved all humanity, Marvin had a profound love for his wife Terre. The story of how they fell in love and then met is more romantic than any work of fiction I've ever encountered. But what is even more beautiful than how he fell in love is how he grew in love. His love for Terre intensified as it matured. I remember how very proud he was recently when he phoned us to tell us that Terre was awarded a research grant of an academic nature, how he rejoiced in her achievements as much as in his own. Marvin was very much a family man. He'd been exceedingly close to his late parents and to his beloved sister of blessed memory. He remained close to his sister Terry's family, to his nephew David who is with us today, and to his cousins, and our children, and our grandchildren. He would usually manage to find time in his extraordinarily hectic schedule to share the Passover seder or High Holiday services with us. Whenever he would give a concert in a city where any of his cousins happened to live, he would provide us with tickets, of course, and then take us backstage afterwards to meet some of the other performers and introduce us proudly as his family. We will always treasure the memory of the time when Marvin took us to Washington D.C. for a concert at The White House and sat us in the front row, just two seats away from President and Mrs. Reagan—he was not partisan, it's okay—he was a chaver tov, he was a loving companion.

And finally came Rabbi Eleazar ben Arach who said "lev tov," a good heart. There is a Yiddish idiom that defies translation. We say of a very special person: he is a "gute neshama." A lexicon will tell you it means "a good soul," but it means infinitely more than that. It is a sublime existential concept; it means someone whose very essence is goodness. We do not use that term lightly. Marvin was ultimately a "gute neshama." That is why he was so universally beloved during his all too brief lifetime. And that is why he will be so profoundly missed.

A century ago the great Hebrew poet Chaim Nachman Bialik, anticipating his own premature death, wrote his own eulogy. It is as valid at this moment as it was then: "After my death, mourn me thus. There was a man, and see, he is no more. Before his time, his life was ended. And the song of his life was broken. Oh! He had one more melody and now that melody is lost forever. Lost forever."

—Rabbi Paul Kushner

ACKNOWLEDGMENTS

I found out that writing a book isn't that much different from writing a song. For when I'm finished at the piano, the music needs lyrics to bring it to life. And so it has turned out to be with *The Way I Was*. I needed collaborators, and, therefore, there are many people to thank.

First is Gerry Gardner, whose contribution was invaluable and whose patience was unending as we kept Federal Express's profits high and our fax machines humming between Los Angeles and New York.

I owe a deep debt of gratitude to Robert Stewart, my editor at Scribners. He gave freely of his time, and forced me to better understand the way I was. I also must thank Denise Yuspeh Hidalgo for her typing and diligent preparation of the manuscript. A special thank-you to Sam Flores for his meticulous proofreading.

I also want to thank again my beloved parents for giving me such a strong sense of family; my sister, Terry, for her understanding; and my friends and relatives for filling in the gaps in my memory.

Finally, thanks to my wife, Terre, for starting me on the road to new memories.

And to you, dear reader, let me say what I said on Oscar night, 1974, "I think we can now talk as friends."

Marvin Hamlisch
New York City, 1992

ABOUT THE AUTHOR

Marvin Hamlisch was a composer and conductor. After attending Juilliard School of Music and Queens College, he conducted the Tony Award–winning *A Chorus Line* and composed dozens of scores for such films as *Sophie's Choice*, *Ordinary People*, and *Three Men and a Baby*. Hamlisch won multiple Oscars for his work in *The Way We Were*, as well as another for his adaptation of Scott Joplin's music for *The Sting*. He received two Emmys for his musical direction of *Barbra Streisand: The Concert*. Hamlisch held positions as the principal pops conductor for symphony orchestras across the country, including the National Symphony Orchestra in Washington, DC.